Opening the Gates of Glory
Volume 1
The Beatific Life

Adonijah Ogbonnaya Ph.D

Opening the Gates of Glory Volume 1
The Beatific Life
Adonijah O. Ogbonnaya, Ph. D.

Opening the Gates of Glory Volume 1 - The Beatific Life
Publications Copyright © 2020, literature arm of AACTEV8 International (Apostolic Activation Network)
Aactev8 International 1020 Victoria Ave. Venice, CA 90291
www.aactev8.com

Published by Seraph Creative
ISBN: 978-1-922428-06-6

Library of Congress data
No part of this book may be reproduced, stored in retrieval system, or transmitted in any form or by any means, electronic, mechanical, photocopy, recording or otherwise except for brief quotation in print review without prior permission from the holder of the copyright.

Scripture quotations from the New American Standard Bible unless otherwise stated. NASB, KJV.

Cover art by Taylor Remington
Typesetting, Illustration & Layout by Feline
www.felinegraphics.com

6	**FOREWARD**
9	**THE BEATITUDES**
11	**INTRO**
13	**Getting to Happy: Blessed is ...**
	Blessed One: Eulogia
	Blessed 2: Makarios
17	**Kenosis**
	A Cosmic Generosity
22	**1 - Empty it all out: Blessed are the Poor in Spirit**
	Poverty of Spirit
	Poor in Spirit
	Kenosis is the key to the Beatific life.
	Out of Nothingness, Create!
	Humility, Love and the Law
	The Beauty of Self-Denial
	The Same Mind As Christ
	Suffering
	Others
	Weakness is Strength
	Fruitfulness and Increase
	For Theirs is the Kingdom of Heaven
48	**2 - Go ahead and Cry: Blessed are they that mourn**
	Depression and Compassion
	God Will Comfort
	The Heart of Miracles
	Fear of Tears
	They shall be comforted
	The God of All Comfort
	Joy Comes In The Morning
64	**3 - Power Under Control: Blessed are the Meek**
	Resolute Disposition

Experiencing Meekness
A Fruit of the Spirit
The Power to Transform the World
Dimensions of Freedom
Meekness as Making Space
Meekness and Contentment
Seek Meek
Sons Of Your Father
The Meek Shall Inherit the Earth

82   4 - Living a Satisfied Life: Blessed are those who hunger
Blessed Hunger?
The Object of the Hunger and the Thirst
All These Things
Benefits of Righteousness
Eternal separation

94   5 - What Goes around Comes around: Blessed are the merciful
Bowels and Brains
Mercy as One of the "Is-ness" of God
The Fulfillment of Purpose
A Divine Attribute
Be Like God
The Choice of Mercy

108   6 - Visional Clarity: Blessed are the pure in heart
The Heart Cannot Be Hidden
Beyond Bitterness
Holy Spirit and Vigilance
Standing Guard
A Key To Eternity
A Descendant of Heaven
The Originator Of Thought and Cosmic Travel
Creating Out of No Thing
Be Free
Olam

    Governing The Worlds
    Know Your Heart
    God is Love
    The Mystic Way
    Love is immortality.
    De-Cluttering
    Creating From Gold
    Pouring Out On The Earth
    A Benediction

136   **7 - Blessed are the Peacemakers**

150   **8 - Blessed are they which are persecuted for righteousness sake**
    Self-Generated Suffering
    Righteousness Generated Suffering
    Justice and Mercy
    The Atmosphere of Heaven
    Ministering To The Unaccepted
    Christ, Our Model

170   **9 - Identified with the crucified: Blessed are ye when men shall revile**

178   **10 - You are in Good Company: for so persecuted they the prophets**

182   **ABOUT THE AUTHOR**

183   **ABOUT SERAPH CREATIVE**

FOREWORD

The Beatitudes are probably one of the most well-known and written about of all the sermons of Jesus.

I wrote this book to discuss my views and interpretation of these important verses to the believer living in the modern era. Having a background in Semitic languages gives me a unique perspective on the native language of the text and an understanding of the undercurrent of the culture at the time. The context of scripture sometimes provides so many shades and shadows of meaning, giving the reader more perspective on the allegorical and metaphorical meaning behind the text.

The traditional interpretation and structure of the Beatitudes is the 8 verses, as structured in the English bible. However, the beatitudes were supposed to be structured as 10 different ideas, or 10 principles, based on the meaning of each verse. The principle of 10 is all over Hebraic culture. The number 10 also means creativity or the creative principle in nature.

Jesus speaks to us today and His words resonate in our hearts. The message He preached on that day, 2000 years ago, is still valid to our world. Jesus' revelation of His kingdom turns our world upside down. This is one of the reasons we still mine this great sermon — to find the hidden gems of meaning and the revelation Jesus seeks to provide to us today.

I trust as you read this book on the Beatitudes, God will give you new lenses to read the scriptures and an even deeper understanding of the words He spoke all those years ago.

Jesus Christ is still the best teacher and preacher who ever walked this Earth. His stories and parables, His well-hidden secrets still confound us today.

These words have given me much comfort and much joy as I studied their meaning and received the revelation from God. I explored the pathways and journeyed with the Holy Spirit to bring you this book, and to help you on your path with Jesus.

Most theologians and scholars would provide you with a commentary or explanations of the words, and definitions of the original Greek and Aramaic texts, with some discussion regarding their interpretation and meaning.

I have taken the less well-worn path of writing my views and understanding in a flowing text, to give you an experience of the atmosphere of the moment, as the words of Jesus washed over the crowd - His meaning slowly dawning on their faces.

I imagine some disciples asked Him many questions afterwards, as is the Hebrew way. I trust this book might answer some of your questions as you follow my train of thought and see the pattern of the scriptures weave an incredible tapestry of God's ways and truth.

Jesus truly brings new values and ideas to a Jewish culture on the precipice of conflict. The Roman world had dominated their promised land. The sound of a nation in turmoil, captivity and being ruled by the gentile, created a cry in the Jewish soul for freedom and emancipation.

Jesus speaks these words into the context and brings hope.

This is not the hope the way humanity defines, this is a hope beyond the temporal, time-bound reality. This hope Jesus offers, is a hope settled on the Kingdom of God.

As you read this book, may the hope of Christ Jesus fill you, and brim over to the surrounding culture.

When Jesus spoke the Beatitudes,
it wasn't purely for a moral purpose.
The Beatitudes are key to the
Heavenly realms and dimensions.

Dr O

THE BEATITUDES

When Jesus saw the crowds, He went up on the mountain; and after He sat down, His disciples came to Him. He opened His mouth and began to teach them, saying,

"Blessed are the poor in spirit, for theirs is the kingdom of heaven.

"Blessed are those who mourn, for they shall be comforted.

"Blessed are the meek, for they shall inherit the earth.

"Blessed are those who hunger and thirst for righteousness, for they shall be satisfied.

"Blessed are the merciful, for they shall receive mercy.

"Blessed are the pure in heart, for they shall see God.

"Blessed are the peacemakers, for they shall be called sons of God.

"Blessed are those who have been persecuted for the sake of righteousness, for theirs is the kingdom of heaven.

"Blessed are you when people insult you and persecute you, and falsely say all kinds of evil against you because of Me.

Rejoice and be glad, for your reward in heaven is great; for in the same way they persecuted the prophets who were before you.

INTRO

We have been talking about Beatitudes, Beatitudes as being gateways into realms of glory. I want you to understand that Beatitudes are powerful, extremely powerful tools, because they are structured according to the principles of the spoken Word of God when He created the Earth. Most Christians read it as eight Beatitudes, or sometimes nine. Actually, there are ten. But Jesus did that deliberately because you always begin with ten; ten, not eleven. Ten fingers. Ten toes. This is the basic principle that God inserted in your body for creativity. Ten fingers. Ten toes. Ten to go. Ten to work.

Getting to Happy: Blessed is ...

Jesus lays out keys of blessing in the Beatitudes, so it's important we understand what He is talking about. The Greek language used in the New Testament has two words translated "blessed". Since I like Dr. Seuss, I will call them 'Blessed One' and 'Blessed Two'.

Blessed One: Eulogia

"Blessed One" has to do with speaking well of someone or someone speaking well of you. It is speaking a "good word". In the case of the believer, it is God speaking well of the creation and humanity. This is where Scripture uses the Greek word *eulogia*. (The same source as the English term "eulogy", when we speak well of the dead at a funeral). Eulogia is often used as our response to God's expression of goodness to the creation, especially human beings. It grows from the Divine idea that the world is good, which in itself flows from the reality of the goodness of God.

> *Blessed be the God and Father of our Lord Jesus Christ, who has blessed us with every spiritual blessing in the Heavenly places in Christ,*
>
> Eph 1:3 NASB

This word "blessed", used in Ephesians 1:3, deserves particular attention in its own right. However, it is not a word that means "happiness" for we are called to speak well of God even in the midst of our grievance against God. Eulogia is not based on human emotion, experience or sentiment. Rather, on the character of God. This is an act of faith, which rests on the fact that God is good.

With this blessing, you are saying "No circumstance in my life is final. I defy that temporality is eternal." Blessing those who hurt you moves you from existence to eternity. Eulogia blessing is an ontological position — because of who you are you cannot help but speak well of people. You have a certain level of contentment from being in God, despite your circumstances. From here you can speak well into all situations.

Blessed 2: Makarios

However, we are focusing here on the wisdom, power and secrets of the Beatitudes. This is a different type of blessing. In Matthew 5, we encounter "Blessed Two", from the Greek word "*makarios*". This means "to be happy", usually in the sense of receiving privilege or favor from another because of how one has carried themselves.

As a Christian, *eulogia* comes from your state of being, *makarios* comes from your attitude. You are as happy as you want to be.

However, if you focus on the privilege to be received, you forgo the happiness it means to bring. In fact, by focusing on the happiness as your goal, you kill it.

Happiness is a way of seeing and judging or evaluating our circumstances. Judging a circumstance and looking at goodness and badness in terms of how it affects us determines happiness or unhappiness. Ultimately, at least based on what I have learnt from the Beatitudes, it is not the experience of a thing or circumstance that should determine happiness. Thus, "happiness" is not feelings. The excitement, passion and ecstasy that grows from an act or situation from the moment of its full moon is not what inspires happiness.

I must point out that I am not equating happiness with joy (Greek; *chara*). While happiness is the attitude we take inwardly to the situation, joy can be described as the external expression of the inner attitude, which we call happiness, or an outer expression of inner contentment and satisfaction.

Now I know that this goes against much of what has been taught. In the Christian Judaic faith, joy is expressed in worship and at the hearing of good news. The measure of joy is not laughter but the extent of worshipful expression in the presence of the goodness of God. However, this Blessed Two is peace and rest in the infinite sea of God. It is not contentment with what one owns but getting to the place of not grasping for the fleeting non-reality of things.

Even hope can make the heart sick if deferred. The truth is that hope is often deferred. Then to be happy there must be an Archimedean point from where one can look with satisfaction at the chaotic circumstances of life and call it good, as God did in the beginning. I am inclined to believe, based on what I learned from Jesus, that happiness is not the result of good luck or good fortune or even prosperity. Rather, it is the result of deliberate intention and forethought; a decision to look at everything from God's perspective. It is hidden in the deliberate letting-go of the world. One is happy as one wishes and chooses to be. Happiness is a defiance of ennui, defiance of the claim of circumstantial finality, rejection of the false claim of the passing world upon our soul and consciousness.

Jesus inserted Himself in history and changed the narrative. Your well-being does not depend on what people do to you, but the story you tell yourself. Your narrative determines your history.

Kenosis

The concept of "kenosis", the emptying of self, is missing from the West. We are trying to find ourselves. We must remember the kenotic principle demonstrated by Jesus.

2 : Kenosis

> *Let this mind be in you, which was also in Christ Jesus: Who, being in the form of God, thought it not robbery to be equal with God: But made himself of no reputation, and took upon him the form of a servant, and was made in the likeness of men: And being found in fashion as a man, he humbled himself, and became obedient unto death, even the death of the cross. Wherefore God also hath highly exalted him, and given him a name which is above every name: That at the name of Jesus every knee should bow, of things in Heaven, and things in Earth, and things under the Earth; And that every tongue should confess that Jesus Christ is Lord, to the glory of God the Father.*
>
> Philippians 2:5-11 NASB

Jesus, being God, humbled himself to death by human hands! That is true emptying. Then God rewards Him. This is the path of Christian spirituality as laid out by Christ in the Beatitudes, especially the first "Blessed are the poor in Spirit".

A spirituality of self-emptying — to pour out oneself into the world so one is free to act according to the patterns of God. Your whole being is dependent on something and someone other than your self, circumstances and actions.

You cannot be your own savior. Your "will" cannot be your idol. Good things cannot be your idol. The "I" idol will capture you and prevent you from going where you need to go. A Christian is an "iconoclastic" being. A shatterer of idols. God does not force emptiness on anyone. It is a deliberate, free choice. A willing self-emptying. The person who does not willingly self-empty can not create anything (even the creation of evil).

Kenosis is a willing outflowing and emptying that does not leave us empty. The Christian may fear that if they empty themself, they may become nothing. The Hebrew understanding is not that you become "nothing", but that you become "no thing". God poured himself out in Creation, yet remained full. Jesus poured himself out, yet he did not stop being God. It allowed our inclusion in Christ.

Could it be that the reason Christians are having problems is that they are "full of themselves"? Now, kenosis is not humiliation. It is not being walked over. This is not "I am a useless sinner who does nothing right". Rather, you are an ever-flowing fountain that is emptying themselves into vast arrays of worlds, new creations and created channels of God's love into the world.

Other religions claim there is no self. There is a self. In fact, we have created many selves that behave differently in different situations. The real you has been subsumed by culture, education, family and fears.

All the selves you are struggling with are not you. They bring confusion. However, there is an image and likeness to God, to which you must become acquainted, a true inner relationship.

The real ground of your being is in you but many selves are being projected, fighting over things which are not even important to the true you.

A Cosmic Generosity

Kenosis is a powerful phenomenon for the believer. It is the basis for a cosmic generosity.

The word cosmic is not new age. It's scriptural. Your whole being is interconnected to every part of creation and from your being, life is poured out to everything that exists. The Divine in a believer is poured out on the thirsty tongue of creation. Empty to receive new content. Emptying self-creates. If the cup is full it cannot receive new content.

Jesus emptied himself of his deity, reputation and power (e.g. He didn't call down angels to defend Himself). Empty spaces are vital.

The Beatitudes are the key to kenosis, the key to self-emptying, especially the first Beatitude.

1ST BEATITUDE

1st Beatitude, Empty it all out: Blessed are the Poor in Spirit

Blessed are the poor in spirit, for theirs is the kingdom of Heaven.

Matthew 5:3

There are two types of poverty in Scripture. Poverty **of** Spirit and Poverty **in** Spirit.

Poverty of Spirit

Pride is poverty of spirit — to be full of themselves, as Jesus pointed out in Revelations 3:17: "... *you say, 'I am rich, and have become wealthy, and have need of nothing,' and you do not know that you are wretched and miserable and poor and blind and naked...*" (NASB)

> The kenotic lifestyle is a selfless lifestyle.

This church has placed the "I" in the center where God ought to be and made material possession the measure of spirituality. It says, "I have need of nothing" which speaks to self-enclosure and the inability to Love. It knows nothing beside itself and thus feels threatened by every passing wind. It knows not its true inner nature. It is possessed by a lack of self-knowledge. Poverty of spirit is clearly seen where the "I" is the false king and sets itself up for rebellion over what God demands. The works of the flesh are signs of this poverty of the spirit. In all works of the flesh listed by Paul, the person is seeking to fill the void. **Kenosis** is the deliberate outpouring which engenders life while **void** is unproductive and unrelenting chaos with contrived activities which in the long run leaves one depleted, unsatisfied and unfulfilled (Genesis 1 calls it *tohu wa-bohu* (תֹהוּ וָבֹהוּ). Kenosis is a void that brings life. Works of the flesh end in a void that is Hell, that takes and takes without giving anything back.

If you are "full of yourself" you are empty of all that is truly good and Divine. Self-emptying is where Christian growth and life begins. Christ is our archetype and template. Kenosis is a "Christo-genetic" principle position. We do not measure by our standards and culture, but only by Christ. Through kenosis, when we say "I", we are truly saying "Christ", as Paul revealed.

> *I have been crucified with Christ; and it is no longer I who live, but Christ lives in me; and the life which I now live in the flesh I live by faith in the Son of God, who loved me and gave Himself up for me.*

Galatians 2:20 NASB

We cannot use a false I, an ethnic I, a cultural I, religious or denominational I. Christ is the only measure.

It is out of no thing, that God created the world. Not "nothing", as He was there. He created out of "no thing".

The Incarnation is kenosis. God became a human being. That is an emptying of self-will. Self-will says "I will not allow anything to function separate from my fabricated I. The I must assert itself with whatever it comes into contact, maintaining the same understanding and processes that are killing it".

Kenosis is the antidote. Those who enter Kenosis determine the cause of universal events. They are open to eternal possibilities and resources.

Poor in Spirit

Poor **in** spirit, as Jesus spoke in the Beatitude, is the revelation and understanding that I own nothing. No thing belongs to me. Owning is conforming all we contact to our fabricated temporal ego. Emptying ourselves opens ourselves to the eternal Kingdom of Heaven.

The kenotic lifestyle is a selfless lifestyle. Emptying into selflessness. We do not mean we are non-existing, conscious-less entities, without God's image. Instead, it is a heart posture of continual reliance on God, to be filled by him. Self-emptying enriches us, it does not impoverish us.

It is a letting go of the illusion of the temporal realm and all the chance and falsehood it seemingly imposes on the Divine within us. We must empty as if we know nothing, become powerless, foolish and fleeting in material ownership. "Possession" is a good term. We possess what we own, similar to a demon. We have put some of ourselves into it. Everything we possess becomes our master.

We must learn the utility and value of material objects yet remain detached. Attachment is the problem here. We are attached to our words. If someone does not believe us, we get upset. We get attached to our emotions, our clothes, our reputation, our ministry, our things. Religion is the greatest possessing tool on Earth.

We cannot change our circumstances, we can not activate what is deeply embedded in us. This demonic false I must go so the true Divine self may be "all in all". Until "It is no longer I that live" but Christ — the foundation of all creation, who holds all things together, the one who grants us His Divinity, who laid down his life for us — becomes the true and only I in us.

Christ in us makes a people that can feed the universe, flow life into uncreated and darkened aspects of creation and truly carry redemption and salvation.

If we want to kill those who differ from our I, we are full of something that is not Christ. If your politics makes you forget your Christianity, then you are full of something that is not Christ.

Kenosis is a technology. God says "I am going to put as much as I Am into you, but you must pour yourself out first". We know that how the church is functioning is not how it is meant to be. Self-emptying and detachment from this world does not mean you'll be poor. Actually, the emptier you are in Christ, the more you qualify to govern over wealth. The more you attach yourself to money, the less you qualify. The more you attach yourself to Earthly love, the less you will have. You will crave receiving, and not giving. You will not participate in the promise of "*Give, and it will be given to you. They will pour into your lap a good measure — pressed down, shaken together, and running over. For by your standard of measure it will be measured to you in return.*" (Luke 6:38 NASB)

Pour yourself into the world and God will pour into you. That is what Jesus did. It is who you truly are. Someone much greater than the I you are currently projecting. When you know this true self, you will stop fighting the fights and fearing the fears that you do.

Kenosis is the key to the Beatific life.

Now you can see the foundation of Christianity is the kenotic principle as manifested when God became man. It is the self-giving of God, the outreaching love of the Divine with which he pours himself into creation. This is the emptying which we find in the famous Philippians 2 passage mentioned above.

Jesus lays out the path of Christian spiritual practice as being the cultivation of a self-emptying lifestyle. The essence of Christian life, worship and practice is to embody humility — that is an out pouring of the self to God and to others. Seeing one's self from the perspective of self-emptying is to understand that one's whole being is dependent on something or someone beyond one's physical and even spiritual powers. For one to channel Divinity and receive the blessedness of which our Lord Jesus speaks, there must be such humility which sees oneself compared to the awesome vastness of God's being as being "no thing".

It is true that there is no emptiness forced upon us by God. In Christ, we see a willing self-emptying. This willing outpouring forms the basis of authentic spirituality and creativity. When we come to grasp the fact that "all is of God" as the Psalmist said, then we come to the state of outflowing an emptiness that does not leave us empty, a self-emptying in which we remain full and content with Christ as the archetypal self.

As previously stated, I doubt very much if this state of being "poor in spirit" can be equated with humility in the sense of "humiliation" — of thinking of oneself as useless or even pathetic — but rather of being an ever-flowing fountain which is forever emptying itself into vast arrays of worlds. In this sense, the Christian assumes that there is a content to the human being which the non-enlightened may seek to grasp to their own destruction. It is understood that one has no independent self, no wealth, no health, and no righteousness without God as the ground of being. Jesus put it this way *"without me you can do nothing"* (John 15:5). There is in Christianity a "with me," a God content, an image, a likeness with which man must become acquainted and understand (understand-relational mode of being). It is knowledge of this content and its awesome nature that makes "self-emptying" a powerful phenomenon. So, there are several things involved in the self-emptying of which we speak (a cosmic generosity in which the Divine in man is poured out). Empty yourself: if the cup is full, then it cannot receive new content.

To create a world God created an empty space, to form a child the woman's womb was created an empty space as a place of possibility. Thus, before Christ could take on human nature, he had to empty himself of his self-consciousness, reputation and deity. Continual emptying of self by all means necessary is the key to unlocking your infinite possibility. Modes of emptying include praise, thanksgiving, love, compassion, generosity and sacrifice. Everything that flows later on in the Beatitude springs from this fact of self-emptying — being "poor in spirit." The mourning, peacemaking, meekness, righteousness, mercy, purity, perseverance in persecution, Holy silence in the face of abuse and extreme joy in extreme circumstances all flow from this one attitude. They are fruits of non-attachment to self.

Out of Nothingness, Create!

So, emptying the self is where the path to Christian spirituality and Christ-centered enlightenment and growth begins. When we are empty, we approach another person or situation with the Christ-made design template, and with Christo-genetic presuppositions with which all must be measured and how it must turn out. We must approach the temporal and the eternal with this nothingness, for it is out of nothing that God created the world. Here is the incarnation principle; God becomes man, being found as man he emptied himself. We must overcome self-will. Self-will says, "I will not allow anything to be arranged or function independent of "I". When we are full of the "I" the "I" must assert, absorb or annihilate whatever it comes into contact with. But when we are full of God, we enrich, gladden, fulfill and advance the other toward its Divine destiny. The antidote for this arrogance of the "I" is self-emptying. Those who can master emptiness determine the course of universal events because they become open to eternal possibilities. This poor in spirit means that one abides in the state of "own-nothing". Owning is the process of conforming all that we meet to our fleeting self-image. In this state, we free ourselves to be open to the Kingdom of Heaven.

We spend our lives trying so hard to maintain the self that is so elusive. When we fall into God, we come to the realization that, without God, what we call self is nothing but a question mark, a void, nothingness. The kenotic life is a selfless life. Again, by this emptying out into selflessness we do not mean that we are not here as conscious entities and that God did not create us in His image. It is a posture, an attitude of unconditional surrender to God which engenders a blessedness. This is the letting go of our ego. Our ego is in reality the imposition of the illusive nature of the temporal, the imposition of chance and falsity on the Divine image within us.

> In knowledge we must become as though we know nothing

In knowledge we must become as though we know nothing, in wisdom we must become as foolish, in power we must become as powerless understanding the fleeting nature of all which we hold dear. We must be converted as to be like a baby, *nepios* — wholly dependent on God. Until we cease to be what we so often call "ourselves" (which in most cases is not our true Divine self) we cannot be like God as the ever-open possible present. So much of what we experience in the world ends up creating a false self — a self in opposition to God, the world and others. But this "I", this demonic façade, must cease to exist so that the greater "may be all in us." We must come to the place where Paul came to where he had to accept that "'I' no longer live, but Christ (the original Divine self) lives in me" (Gal 2:20). The "I" must now live by the self-emptying faith into the Son of God, who in His outgoing effulgence of humanity coming from God, empties His plenitude daily to make a way for us in Himself and the world.

There are so many things with which we fill ourselves. These things we often mistakenly equate with who we are. In so doing we make ourselves unfit for the entrance of the new being and of the new aeon (age). We fill ourselves with laws, rules, ideologies and forms of idols.

> *For through the Law I died to the Law, so that I might live to God... I do not nullify the grace of God, for if righteousness comes through the Law, then Christ died needlessly.*
>
> Galatians 2:19, 21 NASB

The law is not evil. In fact, it is good at its very core. When we come to it with a full self which assumes that we can keep it, rather than filling us with God, it fills our self-righteousness. When the Law, rather than the Giver of the law fills us, we end up creating more and more rules and taboos which bind and entangle us. We suffocate ourselves. It is the fact that we come to the law with the assumption that we can perform it by ourselves that overloads and crushes us. This endeavor fills us with the 'not-God'. The law stares us in the face and says, "You cannot keep me. You may fill yourself with me, but I am not the one you need to fill you. You will over-exert yourself unto death if your focus is to use me as a way to God. If you fill yourself with me you shall be left empty and frustrated for you cannot keep me." The Bible does not say, God is law but "God is Love," (1 John 4). It tells us that "love is the fulfillment of the law," (Romans 13:10).

The thing about love is that it is known not by possession but by the emptying of self into others for good. The more we empty love out the more of it we seem to have. It is interesting that we use the phrases like "keep," "obey," and "break" when we speak of law but words like "show," and "give" as verbs of fulfillment for others when it comes to love. It is when we die to or empty ourselves of the legalism of the law that we really begin to love God.

The law itself can be another god filling us in such a way that the true God has no place within us. In the incarnation we see God refusing to be an idol even to Himself. For without the self-emptying of God into creation, we will find no place and without the self-emptying of God into humanity we will not be Divine in any sense of the word. Grace is the emptying out of our presumed ability to keep the law so that God can be poured into a sinner to make them whole before God's awesome holiness.

We fill our lives with all types of things. We fill ourselves with idols of all sorts. This theme of self-emptying calls for an iconoclastic stance towards every idol made by man, including the idol that is human being.

One of the idols with which we fill ourselves is materialism.

The Beauty of Self Denial
[Greek word **apheken** (ἀφίημι) which means to "let go"]

Emptiness implies self-denial. Selflessness is partially the fruit of self-denial. Thus, "poor in spirit" speaks to the principle of self-denial.

> And He summoned the crowd with His disciples, and said to them, "If anyone wishes to come after Me, he must deny himself, and take up his cross and follow Me."
>
> Mark 8:34 NASB

Self-denial is self-emptying that leads to fearlessness. "Poor in spirit" then means that one comes to be at rest and is carried along in the rest by the river of God. Being rich in spirit is equivalent to "poor of spirit." It is a direct contradiction to our over-anxious modern existence which seeks personal possession as the ultimate expression of the self. Note the very word possession is also in the idea of being taken over by a foreign entity. This modern sickness even equates personal possession with spiritual health. It is at the root of idolatry. But if one pays close attention to the Lord, we hear Him say to his brothers the Pharisees *"If you were blind, you would have no sin; but since you say, 'We see,' your sin remains."* (John 9:41 NASB) And again, to the early church *"Because you say, "I am rich, and have become wealthy, and have need of nothing," and you do not know that you are wretched and miserable and poor and blind and naked"* (Revelation 3:17 NASB)

They were caught in the web of personal possession and ownership. Those who are poor in spirit see what they have as belonging to the Lord and avoid seeing it merely in terms of personal possession. They understand that *"The Earth is the Lord's, and all it contains. The world, and those who dwell in it."* (Psalms 24:1).

> All experiences of our so-called reality are fleeting

This refusal to be attached to the temporal material world is the foundation for the miraculous. It releases the universe to do what it was meant to do for us. The world must be for God what God created it to be. It is only in this way that the world can be freed to be for us what it was created to be. This is one of the ways in which the world produces its increase and plenty for us. In this self-emptying release of the world we, in a sense, invest it into God who, in mutual self-emptying, releases it back to us.

> *And Jesus answered and said, Verily I say unto you, There is no man that hath left house, or brethren, or sisters, or father, or mother, or wife, or children, or lands, for my sake, and the gospel's, But he shall receive a hundredfold now in this time, houses, and brethren, and sisters, and mothers, and children, and lands, with persecutions; and in the world to come eternal life.*
>
> Mark 10:29-30 (KJV)

What is important here is the Master's use of the Greek word *apheken (ἀφίημι)* which means to "let go" — the same word that is used in the concept of forgiveness. One act that can put you on the way to happiness is this letting go.

Not until we let go of our ego-consciousness and the fear and anxiety which it releases within us can we be wholly free and ready for God's manifestation. The mistake that so many believers make, especially today in relation to self-emptying, is rather than leaving ourselves in the position of this positive emptiness, we envision a self who is more grandiose than the self which we are supposedly letting go. This is a flawed view in which kenosis is seen in terms of immediate self-aggrandizement through personal effort. Of course, because the motive for such self-emptying is still full of the self, eventually it ends up in "poverty of spirit" — and not "poverty in spirit" which releases blessedness. Jesus is simply calling us to cease from dealing in "possessions" and thus demonizing everything that we touch, including God as if we have personal ownership of them. In this we must also overcome the conceptual frames in which we have placed Divinity and made it difficult for people who do not think like us to touch and taste Him except through our mouth.

We must see the present world in its passing away as the Apostle John insisted on telling us. While we Christians eschew the word "illusion" we nonetheless must come to grips with the Biblical idea that all experiences of our so-called reality are fleeting. Our only real experience of reality is the Divine (God) who is in the business of making all things new. Old things have not only passed away, they are "passing away" even as we experience them. We live in spiritual delusion if we hold on to them, either as it relates to the past or to a future that we can grasp by our thought or strength. If we walk in this kenotic emptiness, we will recognize that everything that happens to us in the "now" will, in the next moment, be no more. We acknowledge that we are nothing without God. Even time, in which we place so much stock, the Bible says, "time shall be no more." To assuage this bondage of time Ecclesiastes tells us that God has *placed eternity in their hearts* (Eccl 3:11). We must awaken in the eternal realm and to do this we must continually empty ourselves of all this fallen world's delusions. As we allow God to release us from the bondage to this world, we attain wisdom a certain kind of ecclesiastical wisdom, wherein we see the vanity of all Earthly reality.

It is in freeing ourselves from the world that we become rulers of the world. When we surrender ourselves to God and let go of our attachment to fleeting of thoughts, ideas and philosophical constructs and the over-emphasis on "I" can God act as God in us. In being poor in spirit, we release the purity of Divine presence devoid of the obstacle of the possessive or possessed ego. How do we do this? The Lord says, *"you shall know the truth and the truth shall make you free."* We must know the truth of the vanity of the world and the emptiness of life without God to free ourselves. Every conditioning of the self from our childhood forces us to forget the true nature of the human person. Even our prayers often mask the desire to fill ourselves with things. We need to experience the full life of Christ and to be filled with his mind. To experience this, we need to release almost everything that we have filled ourselves with. We cannot become like our Father if we are filled constantly with the world and the noxious vexation of its fallenness. We empty ourselves and become little children.

Being poor in spirit is essential to spiritual breakthrough. It is iconoclastic in that it refuses to idolize anything, even the good. In the emptying of the self we take seriously the commandment *"thou shall have no other god before me"* and *"thou shall make no graven images neither of things in Heaven, on Earth, in the sea"* (Exodus 20 KJV). This self-emptying is the rejection of man's fallen tendency to "thingify" everything it values. Since our modern world seems to be consumed with not wanting to be empty, not wanting to be "nobody", this poverty in spirit calls for radical rethinking of what we consider to be "somebodiness". Western theologians are so consumed in their quest to preserve what they consider the "human personality."

The Same Mind As Christ

In fact, one of the greatest problems that seems to confront evangelical Christianity is the fear of losing the self, so they go to a great length to protect the human self — even in eternity.

Thus, they assert implicitly that the human, which is mainly the fabrication of temporal experience, is God even though its transiency is so obvious. Whether we are born in riches or poverty, whether we are members of the church, we must understand that this stand of seeing ourselves as nothing without God is important for promoting Christian knowledge and growth. It is essential for our transformation as we read again in Philippians 2: 5-8:

> *Have this attitude in yourselves which was also in Christ Jesus, who, although He existed in the form of God, did not regard equality with God a thing to be grasped, but emptied Himself, taking the form of a bond-servant, and being made in the likeness of men. Being found in appearance as a man, He humbled Himself by becoming obedient to the point of death, even death on a cross.*

The paradox of Christianity is that it teaches us to think in positive proportionality about ourselves, yet it tells us to deny ourselves if we would gain and find it. This especially as relates to our being in the presence of God. We learn this clearly from the simple life of the Master Jesus Christ as narrated in the above passage. We are in fact encouraged to *"Have this mind / attitude which was in Christ Jesus"* which was the mind of self-emptying. His whole life and teachings cannot be understood without this idea expressed in Philippians. True Christian spirituality begins in this Christological mindset which we see in Jesus Christ. Since Christ is the central personality of, and the heart of, the Christian faith, it means that we must examine this posture carefully to understand what the Bible means when it says, *"Have this mind which was in Christ Jesus."* It is this mind which positioned Him as the Son of man for the glory that was laid before him and actually allows him to attain it. Does not the Bible say, *"pride goes before a fall"* and many cases upbraids a haughty spirit? The exact opposite is said of the lowly spirit and meekness of heart *"God exalts the lowly"*.

The whole life of Jesus is a move towards the negation of human self-assertion and obsessive clinging to life in its external forms.

His life is a negation of our obsessive clinging to position, power, feelings of hurt and right to bitterness. The irony of this is that the affirmation of the inner reality of life leads to the increase of the things that make for the good life. On the cross, He silences human pride and arrogance, which raises itself against the knowledge of God. When man comes face to face with God's absolute nature, he must mark himself down. At this point, he must release whatever hold he has of himself and become nothing before the absolute one. No one can do this for him, no one can crucify him/her for himself/herself.

Paul's "*I am crucified with Christ, I no longer live*" is not an excuse from engaging the world by the power of the spirit of Christ but a Christo-pneumatic release of transformative being into the world. Not even the crucifixion of the Lord is sufficient if one will not also place him/herself on the cross and go through a personal crucifixion. It is in this self-denial and kenosis that we established our Divine identity. His identity must be transformed at the cross so can we be exalted with the Master and be seated in the Heavenly places. Again, we must reiterate that this is not a move into non-existence. It is a move towards identifying with the Lord who emptied himself and became the crucified one of Calvary and who, through that process, was highly exalted and given the Name above all names. In doing so we understand the teaching of the master that whosoever loses his life will gain it. This poor in spirit implies for me a life of complete and total transparency before the Father and, as much as possible, before believers.

Suffering

During the last fifty years or so there has arisen in Christendom, a detraction as it were to the person of Jesus Christ as the crucified one. The interpretation of the life and work of Christ have essentially been torn apart from His suffering and His cross. One of the most insidious aspects of this gospel has been the idea that to follow Christ is attended by a public display of wealth and wantonness as sign of Divine favor. The question is not asked "Who is Jesus Christ?" or "What is His way?" The words of Jesus about His journey and the record of His life is ignored and set on a false foundation of non-suffering. When I look at this new doctrine of the non-suffering disciple and non-crucified exalted Jesus, I found in it nothing but false philosophical principles undergirded by human greed. It has made the doctrine of self-denial very unpopular and denied the example of Christ. We have enthroned the very false-self which Christ denied so that God may be exalted as the true self (if you wish). True life expansions come when the self is allowed to cease that God may be "all in all". It is only this way that the true Heaven can be manifested in the human soul. This Beatitude shows us that for God to fill our inner being the self must go. The spirit of the Lord cannot fill a being that is full of self, for the self of man, un-crucified, stands in the way of everything Divine. *"But a natural man does not accept the things of the Spirit of God, for they are foolishness to him; and he cannot understand them, because they are spiritually appraised."* (1 Cor 2:14)

In this text Jesus teaches self-denial as a way of being filled with the Divine life. To say that Jesus is the epitome of Divine life in human from is even an understatement, for being the highest He became the lowest, being the strongest He became the weakest, being the wisest He appeared the foolish, being the most holy He became sin, being God, He became human. In this blessedness of the poor, we are called to place Christ before us in truth and to become so transparent before the crystal lake of Heaven so that we are formed into the likeness of the Divine life.

> Holy Spirit comes to dwell in us

This pouring out of the self, this "blessed are the poor" attracts Heaven and yes, a witness to those who do not know him. As this poverty of spirit makes us more transparent before men and before God, the Holy Spirit comes to dwell in us so through and through that people can now see God clearly. As the master said, "that men may see your good works and glorify your Father who is Heaven."

This principle goes to the heart of the human ego-focus. It is our common tendency to justify the false-self that has been built up by tradition, customs and fear before God and before man. When we are accomplished and when we feel superior it is hard not to resort to self-glorification. "Blessed are the poor in spirit" reminds us that only in the letting go of the self and coming to God and making God, rather than ourselves, the center, that the Kingdom of God becomes ours. It is only in pure Christian spiritual transparency that true growth is our life. Thus, in this mode of being and living we let nothing come between us and God and our fellowship with one another. We thus become naked before the Lord and not ashamed as children before their parents. We let neither shame nor pride overshadow our transparency before God the Father.

Letting go of this self-consciousness that is a result of the eating of the fruit of good and evil we move and relate to those outcast and the fallen on the periphery as we grow in this transparency. In becoming "poor in Spirit" as Christ we manifest God in the world and thus become instruments of Divine flow and human transformation. We see the Kingdom, enter the Kingdom and inherit the Kingdom of Heaven.

Since we are the temple of the Lord, we need to meditate on this simple principle in order to transform our prayers and worship into a truly Divine experience. In creating conscious poverty of spirit, we do not seek to become non-existent. Rather, we seek to gain proportionate perspective on the nature of the world which so often is tied to an apparition we call "self." By taking on this poverty of the spirit of which our Lord speaks and releasing ourselves, we may come to find it easier to focus and to gain a more expansive and abundant life which is grounded in what is truly real and eternal. So, to be poor in spirit is to detach the self from the passing fancies of this world yet at the same time to engage the Divine with our whole being. This is a freedom being enclosed by ethnicity, traditions, ideology, and interpretive schemes and thought patterns that seek to displace the fluid dynamicity of God. It is not so much that "I am not" but that "God is" the one in the center of my heart and my self-giving.

Others

When we undertake to be poor in spirit, we undertake to humble ourselves before God and one another. So being poor in spirit is seen in reference to our willingness to receive the gifts which God and others bring into our lives. The Christ call to poverty in spirit maybe understood in the context of our personal expansion by being open to the ever presence of the gift of God that comes to us in everyone whom we meet. It should never be looked at in a manner in which we see ourselves as "nothing" that is as lacking what Kierkegaard called "possibility". This is not a call to hopelessness and giving up on God or even ourselves. Rather, it is a call to see the possibility which is inherent for us in the God with whom we have come into relationship.

The point of this Beatitude is Christ pointing to His own self-emptying life as an example of what our stance should be if we want to expand our life in the context of eternity. This is not a call to stay aloof and to judge the world mainly in terms of some sort of negative impossibility. This is a call to love God and neighbor more than self. It is this act of love that causes expansion of spirit and an abounding extension of Christ towards the world. This poverty of the spirit is staring into Divinity which, though it does not ignore the inwards look, nevertheless understands life expansion and abundant life calls for an extension of thought, imagination and love beyond ourselves.

Embodied in this Beatitude is the Christian vision of love for others. There can be no true "love" where the self of the other is placed in absolute control. Our understanding is informed by this self-emptying God who, though self-existing, places Himself in a place of vulnerability. Thus, to say, "blessed are the poor" is something of an incomplete sentence without what the blessedness is pointing to. Christ Himself points that we do not release ourselves in outpouring just for the sake of pouring out. This "poverty in spirit" is the potentiality of revelation and purpose. The statement "blessed are the poor" make sense only in the fact of what it sets in motion, the inheritance of the Kingdom of Heaven. We love not for the sake of loving but the end goal of transformation. We read *"for God so loved the world that he gave"*. Had the statement stopped there it would be incredibly futile for it would enclose God in some sort of impossibility. But the statement continues this way *"that whosoever believes shall not perish but have everlasting life."* (John 3:16 KJV)

Poverty in spirit is not a negation of one's worth; it is placing of oneself in the presence of God and making room for others before God.

Weakness is Strength

In the language of Paul, we hear him say *"When I am weak, then am I strong."* Such posture of weakness makes our ego very uneasy and, like Paul, we often cry vehemently to the Lord that it might be removed. But the removal of the anguish that comes from this posture would result not in the increase of grace (gifting) but in the depletion of grace. The sufficiency of the grace of Christ is revealed evermore as clearly as we submit under the burden of this self-emptying posture in Him. This poverty in Spirit may cause us to come under all sorts of pressure but again it helps us not to forget our total dependence upon God. When we understand that this poverty, this weakness, this seeming marginalization which we suffer comes with blessedness then we glory even in the presence of persecution. Certain infirmities, tribulations, persecutions and attacks that come to us are meant to help us empty ourselves and become more like Christ. Being poor in spirit is a posture of weakness which reveals the strength of Christ. When we are weak by this outpouring of the self, we are strong in Christ.

> Crucified with Christ

The spiritual state of being poor in spirit is one that must be cultivated through intentional awareness. In our interaction with other Christians, we must be intentional and avoid the sad mistake of having our hurts serve as the spiritual framework of our response to crises. Our emotions are often grated at such levels by things which are obviously not good. We must strive to exist under a high degree of the Spirit's influence so, even if we are regarded as weak, Christ will still be glorified. In this self-emptying one is completely enclosed by, and overtaken by, a perception of God's undeserving favor, understanding that God owes him nothing and that God will be completely righteous even if God were to deal with one contrary to all human rationality. In this simplicity of self-emptied stance, one chooses to justify God and to consult God's sovereign wisdom, choosing not to lean on one's creaturely understanding at all. One lays oneself in the hands of God as a lump of clay, letting God mold every fiber into whatever God deems right and good in his sight. Another phrase in the scripture is "*crucified with Christ.*"

In this crucifixion of self, the self-emptied one is completely dead to self-assertion, self-dependence and self-preservation. This state of weakness carries high spiritual seed that can transform even the hardest of rocks. This poverty in spirit, this self-emptying, this renunciation of self, is a spiritual state of mind that we are called to cultivate. This poverty in spirit is medicine needed for the sickness of mind which has overtaken post-modern human beings. Modern man and his offspring in the post-modern world has worked so hard to lift himself up from the dust of his confusion to what is hoped will be Heaven but rather has reached into the straw of Hell's wasteland. He has been emptied not of self but of God and stripped not of serpent skin which has covered his nakedness but stripped naked and bare of true spirituality (been made spiritually naked and bare of true spirituality). In his quest for spirituality on his own terms has become spiritless. Laid out in the dust, not of repentance but of false self-righteousness, of meaningless inclusivity of false tolerance and materialism. Full of himself he is not safe. Such posture created by his philosophies has been hedged by great, great loss of hope. Only in embracing this simple Beatitude can he find medicine for his poverty "of" spirit.

Human beings in this post-information world still seek to save themselves by filling themselves with the false plenitude of artificial things. But Salvation itself, from the Biblical perspective, begins at the place of letting go of self and accepting that in ourselves, as made up by tradition, we are unable to save ourselves. But this is not possible for any human being until he or she comes to an end and sees himself or herself in light of the majesty, purity, love, power and awesome nature of God. As such, this spiritual poverty can be very painful and disheartening since the sword of God strikes at the heart of that which we hold dear. It is this posture that led Paul to cry out "Wretched man that I am! Who will set me free from this body of death?". This also led Isaiah to cry out *"woe is me for I am undone."* This led Isaiah to cry out "Woe is me, for I am ruined! Because I am a man of unclean lips, And I live among a people of unclean lips; For my eyes have seen the King, the Lord of hosts." (Is 6:5). It also led Peter when faced with the majesty of Christ after his resurrection to cry out *"depart from me for I am a sinner."* Believers to whom Christ has revealed the depth of his Divinity and who have seen the depth of human loss come to the place where they see their own poverty in spirit and come to a point of despair and may have to face the dark night of the soul.

Fruitfulness and Increase

This poverty in spirit is the seed of fruitfulness and multiplication in all areas of life, where you witness great spiritual enlargement. Inquire and you will find that the fruitfulness is in proportion to the spiritual poverty. If the sense of spiritual poverty is shallow, the spiritual enlargement will be small also. If the expansiveness of spirit is great, the man or woman will inform you that such enlargement of spirit has come in direct proportion to experience of poverty in spirit which had been undergone. Only those who have felt this poverty which the Lord here narrates know it. This cannot be taught but comes only by experience. When the carnal mind is told these things, it will tell you how unreasonable it is to expect this beatific expansion to proceed from such experience of poverty. If you will see the power and the expansiveness that burst from this poverty in the spirit, you must learn to use the inner eyes enlightened by Christ who spoke these words. It is those who are poor in spirit who discover the treasures hidden in the Heavens which few men find.

Enlargement, expansiveness, spiritual fecundity, a rich and overflowing life in Christ is communicated from the heart of God to those who are willing to drop their eyes and tell you what they have found when they looked into the nothingness that is themselves, what height they have grasped as they sank to lowest and how having sank into the bottomless of Hell they have been raised to the highest. How, having been driven to despair on ever attaining their own salvation, they fell into the arms of Christ and were saved. This Christ-engendered poverty in spirit is a great treasure house in which those who have it, or are driven by it, attain as their inheritance Christ Himself. While it may seem that those who have it have bitter experience of pressing alone unto Christ and renouncing what is seen, releasing all they seem to possess and casting their all upon Christ — so that He may be their all. This poverty in spirit takes away the poverty of soul or spirit which, often disguised by materialism, leaves one empty. The revelation of the Divine self and its possibility that such a man sees when God becomes His riches in Christ sets his soul afire with passion and necessitates a view of the world as possibility of possibilities.

From what has been said above it should be understood that we are not talking about poverty mentality, a kind of self-loathing and reveling in lack in which one feels they deserve nothing wonderful from God. Some believers even today still insist that to be poor in spirit it is necessary to be a pauper and that somehow the lack of worldly well-being is equivalent to being poor in spirit. The fact that Jesus gives the answer to this poverty as the "Kingdom of Heaven" is a sign that this poverty in spirit is the seed for abundant life and Divine overflow. This Spiritual attitude of "absolute dependence" on God which attaches no ultimate value to the false self or supposed absolute claim of material possession is the key to Divine overflow.

We learn this from Job. In his case, God's goal was to cause Job to be the embodiment of poverty in spirit. The goal was to prove that only God mattered to Job and when Job had proved his possession of God, he came into overflow. Even Job's friends and his response to them implied that before Job understood spiritual poverty, he was haughty and self-righteous. A kind of caretaker of Divine gifts is implied in this "poverty in the spirit", so that one sees all that is given to one as an entrustment, from the breath of life to the physical body, from intense thought to wondrous flight of imaginations and creativity. All these are given in this world as instruments for Divine worship and Divine manifestation.

As trustees of God's gifts, one must manage them and direct them to the honor of God. All that one possesses is given as organs for Divine worship. These things ought to be released as needed by The Lord who entrusted them to us. This seeing of all we have as entrusted mediums of Divine worship (service) and not an end in themselves entails that they are for the care of the self and the world. The fact that they are to be use as organs of worship prevents us from abusing them. Again, poverty in spirit delivers us from idolizing these mediums and perceiving them as gods in our lives. In viewing all our possessions as instruments or organs of worship we acknowledge God as the source from whom all blessings flow and the pool to which all must flow. Being that they come from God, poverty in spirit keeps us from pining and complaining about what God has privileged us with. Thus, our disposition is one of thankful acknowledgment of Divine benevolence.

This means that we also should be diligent in increasing the growth of our given talents so that we have greater opportunity for the outpouring of love. Getting wealth and possession is not an issue for the child of God. We should seek to be blessed with abundance, but we must also ask ourselves the question: "to what end?". If the sole purpose is satisfying our every whim and lust than we live in perpetual "poverty of spirit". However, if this leads to an expression of Divine magnanimity, then for God's sake, let the wealth flow. Who controls us and who sets the priority of our lives becomes a crucial question in light of this simple Beatitude.

For Theirs is the Kingdom of Heaven

Those who live in the out-pouring of self and the self-emptying magnanimity of Divinity are the ones who are allowed possession of the Kingdom of Heaven. They take in the Divine and pour it out into creation. The master's use of the possessive adjective indicates two things; First, that this Kingdom can be possessed by those for whom God is their fullness and not their ego. Secondly, this Kingdom can be given as a gift to another. This Kingdom belonging to them is uniquely and finely separated from the Kingdom of God in which God stands uniquely as King, and does not share with another.

Now, while self-giving of God to the people of God is clearly articulated in the Bible, God Himself is not seen as that which man can possess as object. Rather, God is that which a man walking in the outpouring of Divine sonship can become!

For example, when speaking of the children of Levi, Scripture explicitly states *"They shall have no inheritance among their countrymen; the Lord is their inheritance, as He promised them."* (Deut 18:2). Understanding this distinction that God makes between the children of Israel as a kingdom and the children of Levi especially as relating to possessing the kingdom will help as we proceed to ask what is the Kingdom of Heaven which these persons are to possess. (That in which all Israel partook as God's people, secondly that in which the priest the sons of Levi partook specifically the sons of Aaron and that to which the Kings partook as the Lord's anointed.)

> God is that which a man walking in the outpouring of Divine sonship can become

This tripartite possession of God and of the inheritance has something to teach us as we look at the distinction between the Kingdom of God and the Kingdom of Heaven. Furthermore, it should help us with the three references to the Kingdom of God which appear in the Beatitude. Generally, when Jesus says that they possess the Kingdom of Heaven, what did they really possess? To understand this, we need to consider what is denoted or connoted by the word 'Heaven' within the scripture and the history of Israel. What Jesus says here is about the possibility of this Kingdom of Heaven by human beings. Heaven in Matthew 5:34 is said to be "the throne of God" which means it is place from which rulership is exercised. It is a place and environment, a space of dramatization of ruling, dominion and authority.

So, if one possesses the Kingdom of Heaven one is given an atmosphere, and environment within and from where one exercises rulership. Such people who are here named will be given an environment within and from whence they can move in power and authority. In fact, when they are thus, they possess the ability to create a Heaven-environment in which God-like acts occur. It carries with it the idea of the capacity to create a "climate" or an environmental nest for incubating Divine power and releasing it to the world. Thus, the poor in spirit are "nested pneumatic-sphere." They are nested potential Heavens waiting for release. I would venture to say that while the Kingdom of God deals with God directly as person (if I may be allowed that metaphor) the Kingdom of Heaven deals with environment really based on the material manifestation of polity and structural process for manifesting the power of God through His people. This is why I think the book of Matthew, which was written to Israel, uses this language rather than the Kingdom of God. But here is the catch-22 — one cannot possess the Kingdom of Heaven until one has entered the Kingdom of God. Heaven can only truly be manifested where God is already King.

> *At that time the disciples came to Jesus and said, "Who then is greatest in the kingdom of heaven?" And He called a child to Himself and set him before them, and said, "Truly I say to you, unless you are converted and become like children, you will not enter the kingdom of heaven. Whoever then humbles himself as this child, he is the greatest in the kingdom of heaven.*
>
> Matthew 18:1-4

Jesus describes the kingdom as leaven which a woman took and hid in three pecks of flower until the whole was leavened (Matthew 13:33). Of course, the woman symbolizes the principle of fertility and fecundity, an incubator environment in which life is formed and sent forth into the world. Leaven (yeast) is that which causes increase in quantity, the little become larger, the small becomes great. The packs of flour into which the leaven is inserted could be seen as the God-principle into which whatever is inserted, no matter how inert, is energized by the Divine dynamism. Thus, it is the completion of the dialectic process which forces the emergence of a new form, the triangular combustion. This making the small plenty and this increase of the little to the great is intrinsic to any Kingdom of Heaven reality. It is seen also in the parable of the mustard seed.

The Kingdom of Heaven, which these poor in spirit possess, is an embodied layer of Divine mysteries. Their inheritance for being "poor in spirit" is access into the Kingdom of Heaven and its mysteries (Matt. 13:11). The Kingdom of Heaven has so many nested and hidden variables whose doors swing open only to those who are poor in spirit. When it is experienced, it confirms the word and promises of God. One can say that within every word of promise given by God is nested the Kingdom of Heaven's dimensional mysteries whose thread is weaved with other deeper mysteries hidden in the infinite nature of God.

(For further understanding on the Kingdom, see the exploration of The Lord's Prayer in my book "A Golden Cord").

2ND BEATITUDE

2nd Beatitude, Go ahead and Cry: Blessed are they that mourn

"Blessed are they that mourn for they shall be comforted" Matt 5:4

Mourning? The Greek word *pentheo*, translated "mourn," means to mourn, grieve, bewail, to feel grief or sorrow, or to experience pain, with the connotation of willing to do so.

Depression and Compassion

In this sense, mourning is equanimity and soberness and does not entail living in despair. Is Jesus saying that we must go about being sad, a sour puss and a kill joy? Obviously not because in counseling His disciples about fasting he specifically tells them that they are not to go about with sad countenance as the practice was in his day. Rather, they are to put on oil and go out with a joyful countenance so as not to draw attention to their spiritual sacrifices. It is out of this bent of the Lord toward a joyful expression of life in God's service that Paul gives the believer what some may consider an impossible injunction "Rejoice in the Lord always; again I will say, rejoice!" (Phil 4:4). So, if this does not mean an attitude of sourness about the world, what then does it mean?

First, it can be seen in terms of the suffering which human beings go through in this world. It speaks to the heart of God for those who suffer in this world. So, whether it is caused by loss, pain or fear, our response is where this Beatitude is directed. May I say again that this mourning is not a kind of living in regret. In a sense, most mourning is the result of our attachment to the things of this world. The mourning that Jesus is speaking of may be distinguished from depression. Crying is a realistic response to the pain which comes from the brokenness of the world. What distinguishes this mourning from the other kinds of mourning is that its wellspring is God's heart. The Bible interestingly does not say "blessed are those who cry." Rather, it emphasizes mourning which, in a sense, cannot truly be done without engaging the heart of God.

Another kind of mourning is the mourning that flows from the posture of internal compassion. Such mourning reveals empathy for sufferers. There is something about these mourners that opens them to the plight of the world. But this empathic bent calls one not to give up on the world and to turn inwardly to confessional hopeless. Rather, such mournful compassion must be accompanied by a view toward a positive remedy which then engenders hope in the mourner and sufferer. Mourning deals with the reality of human suffering and faces it squarely and even experiences all its pain. It opens up a door of release which lets a new wind in to the dark room of pain. Mourning should not stop us from running to master as Mary and Martha did. While in mourning for their brother Hebrew law required that they stay at home and not leave their state of mourning. But when they heard that the Master was in town, though still in mourning, they ran to meet Him.

God Will Comfort

God is called the "God of all comfort". Jesus promised "another comforter". But in spite of the reference to comfort within the scripture there are those who still refuse to be comforted. What are some things that keep us from accepting comfort? Attachment is one of those things. When that which we love is no more, the fleeting, a sense of loss or regressive thought and regret causes us to mourn.

This type of mourning must be distinguished from the mourning in which this blessedness consists. Mourning is not something we associate with blessing. But we read in Psalm 126:6 *"He who goes to and fro weeping, carrying his bag of seed, Shall indeed come again with a shout of joy, bringing his sheaves with him."* This mourning is that companion of the righteous soul as it seeks for the salvation of others. If you are a soul winner you know the sweat and the pain that accompanies the seed of the word, tears that water the desert souls of men for the planting of the gospel seed. What is lost in so much of today's church is this burden for the lost lives of men and women, whose immediate comfort comes from the salvation of the person for whom we weep. Rather than mourn for the plight of those who we believe are on their way to eternal damnation, or for a group that is deprived, marginalized and oppressed, it seems that many in the church rejoice in the message of doom. We ought not to rejoice that our prophetic words of judgment are being confirmed. Rather, we should weep between the porch and altar until judgment is turned away and mercy runs down the hills of Divine justice.

The Hebrew word *ebel* and the Greek *pentheo*, translated "mourning", all point to the same idea of feeling sorrow or sadness at the very deep level of the human soul. But this sorrow is usually the result of great concern, in this case regarding the state of the affairs of God in the Earth. The Lord speaks of cheerfully doing the will of the Father. In fact, He ends this Beatitude with call to rejoice and not be sad. This may mean that mourning stems from the fact that the condition for this joy, the righteousness peace and joy in the Holy Spirit, is not present. So, these blessed men and women mourn for the existing condition in the world which diminishes this blessedness. It implies that if we are to live life on the higher plane then we are to be sensitive, sympathetic, tenderhearted, and alert to the needs of others and the world.

> His care meant that He was never indifferent

The meaning is more clearly understood by the action we take when we react to those going through heartaches or trauma. We stand in opposition mentally and spiritually to the existential constriction which invades human life and diminishes its Divine blessedness. When we have a heart of mourning, we have to a large extent overcome the insensitivity, lack of care, unconcern, callousness and indifference which characterizes the materialistic orientation of the world. This heartfelt response to the suffering and heartache of others is vital to the success of our Lord's ministry. His care meant that He was never indifferent nor did He try to protect his emotions from the suffering of others.

The Heart of Miracles

A life of mourning is not the absence of joy but the tempering of our exuberance in light of the present suffering of others. This compassionate tenderness and willingness to reach out is at the heart of many miracles done by the Lord. We read so often that Jesus was moved by compassion.

> *Moved with compassion, Jesus touched their eyes; and immediately they regained their sight and*

> *followed Him.* (Matthew 20:34)
>
> *Moved with compassion, Jesus stretched out His hand and touched him, and said to him, "I am willing; be cleansed."* (Mark 1:41)

This compassionate care characterizing this blessed mourning is accompanied by a will bent towards the relieving of the suffering of the other. This openness of the will to help as much as one can, to enter into the suffering of another, is at the heart of authentic mourning. It is an internal consideration reaching beyond crocodile tears. It is a being grasped by the plight of another, beyond superficial appearance, an attitude of interior consideration resulting in exterior action.

Fear of Tears

This profound call to enter into the life of another may sound sadistic to those who presume that life ought to be without pain. Some even consider it destructive arguing that God does not intend for us to suffer. Some preaching of today has conditioned many believers to look at anything that brings tears to be a sign of weakness. But this harks back to the patriarchal discomfort with the emotions. It is not so much that people are afraid of pain and suffering but rather the human emotional reaction to it. It is the fear of tears or mourning and the regard of it as if it stands in fundamental opposition to God, human comfort and strength, that serves the callousness with which so many in our world look at the suffering of others.

Comfortable quiescence in which one hides his emotion from being affected by the plight of the world has great cost to the human soul. Tears and mourning are coins whose payment purchases, for those who know how to use it, greater comfort and joy reaching into the depth of the soul. Much more than those seemingly enjoyed for the moment by those who have avoided the discomfort of their own tears and those of others.

Developing a life of meaningful mourning is one way of setting the heart right, to worship gainfully at the altar of the true God. This heart of mourning lays the ground for authentic worship which can help us on our way to attaining maturity in Christ and to participate in his high priestly function. Tears are both the seed and watering that prepares the laborer for the manifestation of fruitfulness. Those who have no tears have not watered the seed which they have laid in the ground. Although such seed may grow they may fail to produce the full increase of which they are capable.

> *For we do not have a high priest who cannot sympathize with our weaknesses, but One who has been tempted in all things as we are, yet without sin. Therefore, let us draw near with confidence to the throne of grace, so that we may receive mercy and find grace to help in time of need. Hebrews 4:15-16*

There are different dimensions to mourning as used here: 1. Crying 2. Agonizing 3. Moaning 4. Groaning 5. Deep sighing. These responses describe the labor of a soul tuned to the heart of God. Those who desire to be like Christ are urged "Strive to enter through the narrow door; for many, I tell you, will seek to enter and will not be able." (Luke 13:24) The Greek word (the same from which we get our English "agony" and "agonize"), translated "strive," means to labor or fight desperately.

Christian mourning comes from various experiences as has already been stated. But for clarification purposes let us list them now.

> A. A desperate need of God; an inner agonizing and longing for the presence of God. A heart-wrenching outreach for God for union with Him. This heart cry is included in this "mourning" that is here included in this Beatitude.
>
> B. Insight into the plight of the soul and its eternal value and the cost of its loss

C. The failure of the church to wield rule and dominion

D. The physical sickness which afflicts humanity

E. The level of destruction that nature under bondage of sins metes out to humanity and creation in general.

F. The human experience of loss which is the result of the fall.

As Christian disciple we are asked to seek God with such passion and depth, with all our heart in order to find God. Our response to Jesus to be led by Him deeper into the mystery of God assumes that we are willing to deal with the exigencies of life and shed the tears that come with it. How amazing it is that a people whose Master entered the depth of the waters of human suffering and pain would seek so much to escape human pain and suffering. The idea of mourning is not that God seeks to torture us but that we should grasp the presence of God at the moment when we could no longer endure it — when we come to the end of our rope. One of many problems in the way we see suffering is that we do not understand that, before our mourning commences, God has already made a way to raise us up. In mourning, it often seems that we are going to go under and never come back up for air. He is there with comfort and life-giving breath so that our mourning finds a release.

In mourning, we are closer to finding God, sometimes more than we are when we are in joy. Mourning is not meant to last forever or to be our undoing, rather it is meant to be a precursor to joy that lasts. Mourning without comfort is a sentence to Hell. God does not sentence His children to Hell. Yet we cannot avoid the fact that a true search for God involves a high price that often brings tears. We need to understand that there is a price for the hidden pearl of life that we seek and heavy tears may flow from our hidden recesses, but the tears will turn to joy. Paul, in speaking of the experience that we need in order to grasp that life, says we must die to self. But dying to self in the Christian paradigm implies resurrection. This laying aside of the self, this denial of the present form of life is sometimes as painful as death and brings mourning. However, it always leads to Divine comfort. Jesus Christ our Lord speaks to the reality of mourning that accompanies discipleship when He says, "For whoever wishes to save his [a]life will lose it; but whoever loses his [b]life for My sake will find it." (Matthew 16:25)

One of man's biggest fears is giving up what he holds dear. This fear comes from anticipated pain that will come from loss. But in the willingness to give up these false refuges and the willingness to mourn for our misguided beliefs, we are able to find peace. This peace we find in nothing other than God. In and through God come true life, great comfort and fulfillment. The great thing about mourning is that it shoots for us as an arrow into the heart of God - it activates Divine intimacy. How can we carry the cross and not feel pain? This pain is necessary in moving us to a place of increase and away from our comfort zone. Ironically, it is this removal from our comfort zone that brings us to authentic comfort and fulfillment. When the Lord tells us to take up the cross and follow Him and to deny ourselves, our response to our pain and the pain of others moves front and center so that we may make the world a better place. The principle of mourning is central to human relief and renewal in the face of suffering. Crosses are not comfortable or convenient — quite the contrary. But they are liberating and more intellectual than emotional, actually, and should manifest in a love of spiritual life and practice. This Beatitude promises comfort to those who mourn.

The Greek word *parakaleo* is much richer. It literally means "for they shall be called for" in the sense of a person being called to a better situation or summoned to receive consolation, as when we call a crying child to come sit on our lap. It also means to be drawn to someone by their caring for us. From this we understand why we should mourn. Since we have within us the dynamic power of God to create our destiny, if we truly long for God we shall come to God. Further, it is a joyful secret of spiritual life that if we yearn for God, He yearns for us. Like the father of the Prodigal Son, He sees us while we are yet far away and comes running to embrace and receive us.

To pilgrims of the spirit, the happy counsel is given to fervently call out in our hearts for God, to be implacable in our demand for communion with Him. He shall surely call for us and draw us unto Himself in His perfect love. As the old hymn says: "Open wide Thine arms of love. Lord, I'm coming home!" That is truly blessed.

This Beatitude does not make mourning as the eternal focus of our relationship with God. Rather, it implies that the meaningful aspect of suffering is that it has a short duration. As psalmist says, "Weeping may last for the night, but a shout of joy *comes in the morning.*" (Psalm 30:4). When we come to desire God so much that any seeming absence pains us to the core and brings tears when the intimacy which can give people life is so absent when meaningful existence is so near to human beings, but they choose the path of meaningless, we mourn. We mourn only until they are brought into the joy of relating with the Father. Our weeping must be mingled and expressed with the unshakable hope that just around the corner there is light and joy from God.

> Comfort does not always mean to take away the reality of the suffering

They shall be comforted

Comfort does not always mean to take away the reality of the suffering, rather it entails the presence of one who walks alongside of the sufferer. So, the use of the word "comfort" is telling. For this is the same word Jesus uses when telling us of the Paraclete, The Holy Spirit, who is to come and walk along us as we travel this valley of life.

The sorrows we experience when we are captive to life's vicissitudes are always harbingers of positive realizations of the Divine impulses. These experiences are geared towards the disentanglement of the things that bind and keep us down from our flight to living an abundant and a fulfilled life. Jesus who says, "happy are those who mourn", is dashing our often-misguided idea that our pain has no relief in the rock of hope. Herein is the wisdom of God, which can help anyone who will listen. Whatever it is that one is going through, the power of the Christian message is *"For I consider that the sufferings of this present time are not worthy to be compared with the glory that is to be revealed to us."* (Rom 8:18)

We must not be like children who do not understand the temporality of mourning and suffering. Although we may have spent many days distracted by suffering, there is a much deeper work being done within us. We are being prepared for a great Divine fulfillment.

The God of All Comfort

Though at the moment these sufferings are hurtful and even distasteful to us, there is always on the horizon of suffering and mourning a Divine comfort and peace. Focus on the one who can turn your mourning into joy, your morbidity to radiance and grace. Let your tears be the lens through which you look beyond your pain and see the coming glory. Understand that nothing can comfort and transmute your pain into joy but the "God of all comfort".

If you see that possibility of this comfort, and understand its inevitability, you will begin to shout even through your tears. If you get that this comfort is already yours, even in the midst of this pain, then your praise will become the thunder spear that releases the rain in the midst of your nimbus clouded sky. Rather than succumb to the temporal as if it were eternal, get to see the God who is already at work in the midst of your mourning to turn it into joy. As long as you just quietly resolve to focus on the God of your comfort, you will get there. Go ahead and shout for joy while you are still in the midst of your mourning, you will get a Divine response and your heart will be healed. As you have been crying, shedding tears, grieving, reaching out for God, showing yourself to be wholly dependent on God, His heart will be moved, and He will call for you. Like the father of the prodigal He will come to you and envelop you with His eternal comfort. Blessed are you who mourn, your Heavenly Father will surely respond to you and bring you into joy everlasting. There is joy unspeakable and comfort for those who have mourned but now have been comforted.

Mourning does not excuse us from worship and adoration of God. One of the greatest temptations of the mourner is the tendency to feel somehow because we have been suffering and tearful, that we are no longer obligated to worship. Yet authentic mourning must be seasoned with worship. Authentic mourning can help us develop a meditative focus, which equips us to worship God in spirit and in truth. It is in this understanding that we put into effect the idea expressed in scripture that we are more than conquerors because, in the midst of suffering and pain, we are able to have a vision of Divine rest and comfort. We are in Christ, intimately connected to Him in the Godhead as sons and daughters. Thus, when we mourn there is an activation within the Godhead of mercy and grace.

In this Beatitude, we are invited to come to the realization that whatever pain the gods of this age may cause us, is not enough to separate us from the love of God which is in Christ Jesus our Lord. We who listen to the Lord Jesus Christ must have a mindset different from this world. This world, out of spiritual pride, refuses to mourn. They would rather flaunt their self-sufficiency in every way, their false religiosity not allowing them to mourn authentically. Only those who mourn authentically, those who enter into this interior engagement of the self in light of the nature and person of Christ, with an intensity which refuses to excuse the left-over smell of the fall, can truly enter into the serenity and rest of the internal paradisaical conclave of Divinity.

Joy Comes In The Morning

In mourning there also arises an uncertainty about what direction to take in order to return to the normal process of life. There is a loss as to the action one should take, often accompanied with the incapacity to respond in a coherently reflective manner.

Comfort is the return to direction and purpose. Here is often much soul-searching which may be laden with guilt and self-condemnation. This mood may not allow one to respond in ways that accelerates movement toward comfort. The inner landscape is often replete with conflicts, uncertainty and frustrations — but this does not mean that comfort is not available. Comfort according to Jesus is always available. But if we understand what Jesus is saying, there is nothing wrong with mourning; however, we must allow ourselves to be comforted. The greatest that can be given to one who is mourning over their sin and failure is forgiveness. The greatest comfort for the destruction of the sinner is salvation. The greatest comfort for bereavement is resurrection. The prospect of comfort alters the basic structure of sorrow and mourning. To accept the prospect of comfort in the midst of our authentic sorrow without judging ourselves requires a genuine understanding of our connection with God as the God of true comfort and compassion. A God, who in his Sovereignty, wills our good even in the midst of what may seem evil.

What are some obstacles to our entrance into the realm of our comfort?

> Comfort is not a search for pity

Now if we imagine a sorrow that is perpetual our hearts will sink, our soul will despair and our spirit will be broken. The Bible states that "a joyful heart is good medicine, but a broken spirit dries up the bones?" (Proverbs 17:22). Jesus assures us that no matter how deep our sorrow there is comfort available. Looking at the structure of the Beatitude it is immediately apparent that mourning and weeping are a passing phenomenon. The Bible assures us that God will wipe our tears away. They are not meant to last forever. Whether it is large or small, significant or insignificant, mourning and weeping always gives way to comfort, sorrow will always give way to joy. There is no consequent experience of human suffering that does not have a Divine salve and balm directed to it. They shall be comforted. It may not be immediate, it may not be tomorrow, but you shall be comforted. Whether the cause of the mourning is deliberate or inadvertent, there is a future comfort factor embedded in it. This comfort is part of the very nature of God. Again, Paul tells us that God is the "God of all comfort."

Mourning will be infinite if one does not have a way to break it by a contrary affirmation, by a refocus of the thought on the goal of the person of God. It is in appropriating another object for one's emotional focus that comfort is allowed to enter. In times of mourning when one is agitated and finds oneself in an unpredictable crossroad, when one's awareness is narrowed by a heart-breaking event, to say that they shall be comforted may seem like trifling with their pain. But Jesus insists that we must know from the onset of every mournful event that we shall be comforted. In this "they shall be comforted", the mourner finds the object of their peace to be God.

This is important, for God is not so much an external object as an internal reality that grounds the person. As such then it is not what is said outwardly that Jesus is referring to. Comfort is not merely an external phenomenon. One can actually stop mourning outwardly but still carry the restlessness of tears and mourning within. As the mourning is not merely external, comfort is the inner flowing movement from the psycho-schematic structures of inner pain and sorrow to the pneumatic-rewriting of the DNA of sadness and sorrow. This results in an inner assurance and peace which have their basis in the nature of God. The paradox of comfort is that we must be open to it even though our whole being seems to reject it and the circumstances say that any comfort is impossible. Yes, it requires faith to want to be truly comforted.

Comfort is not a search for pity, but rather is the speaking of solace and peace into the context of pain. Comfort is the amalgamation of peace, love, hope and joy anticipated in the midst of suffering. These may be amalgamated in various ways:

1. Maintaining an inflow of love in the midst of mourning;

2. A continuous opening to the feeling of sympathy and compassion towards others;

3. A continuous re-activation of beatific memory by a recalling of the benefit of the Divine testimony. Precious acts of God in one's life are kept in front view to remind one of the unchangeable faithfulness of God.

4. Rekindling of hope based on the promises of God e.g. in the midst of loss resulting from the death one may be comforted by the promised hope of the resurrection.

5. A reflective orientation that considers the present plenitude of the overflowing abundance of God's goodness in one's life.

That one is comforted means that one repossesses oneself. One begins to operate from a place of rest. The power of comfort is that it is a return to the unshakable assurance of God's intrinsic goodness.

3RD BEATITUDE

3rd Beatitude, Power Under Control: Blessed are the Meek

Blessed are the meek: for they shall inherit the Earth.

Matthew 5:5

Meekness has been given a terrible and negative meaning in the various dictionary definitions. It is no wonder that it seems to be a disappearing quality among the great men and women of this era.

How will meekness not be seen as something evil in itself when so-called great men and women have seen meekness as the quivering and abject unfortunate dog, abasing himself before a totalitarian mastery of a tyrant. They see the meek as the apologetic, fearful coward, unable to stand before a superior. They seem to others like a tree forced to bow in a storm.

Leo Tolstoy connects "meek" with the idea of martyrdom when he says of one of his characters "like an ox, his head bent meekly, he waited for the blow of the axe which was raised over him." Margaret Drabble sees the meek as sacrificial victims waiting meekly for the knife and the altar of fire. So too, great novelists like Fyodor Dostoevski, Dylan Thomas and Sir Thomas Browne. In fact, at one point in his novel, Sir Thomas Browne quips that "meekness takes injuries like pills, not chewing, but swallowing them down." Even the Masterful Robert Browning sees meekness in terms of weakness so that he is not hesitant to state that a meek one is "as obedient as a sheep." Of course, Nietzsche for whom the three most valuable values are sex, lust and unhindered force, "Meekness and pity are the virtues of the weak, promoted by those who resent the power of the strong. There is no virtue in being meek if one is too weak to be capable of being otherwise" (Thus Spoke Zarathustra; Friedrich Nietzche).

Resolute Disposition

Meekness is a trained calm that becomes a courageous and deliberate heart. In the many variations in which it occurs, such as obedience, it does so with a golden will delighting in inner pleasure and victory, devoid of that bitterness which is often the bane of the less powerful. So, the meek chooses to die free and chooses to obey not out of compulsion (even though the one who commands may be under the delusion that they are the cause of the reaction of the meek). It is the power of the meek, intrinsic in themselves, that makes them act as they choose to act, in the face of death. The disposition to be patient and long-suffering demands great inner and sometimes physical strength.

While everyone does not regard meekness as a virtue, the Bible places great importance on it. Meekness is a quality of strong character and courage, a resolute disposition geared toward modesty and patience, a leaning toward gentleness born of timidity, a cultivated inner ease and focused and intent on peace. Meekness in the biblical Christian sense is a principle squarely opposed to pride and arrogance, egoism, self-exaltation, haughtiness and self-will so common to modern human beings. In a sense, it is at the fundamental level, what is intrinsically lacking in all who oppose God. Meekness and humility are not hallmarks of weakness as has often been portrayed by the world.

The Bible makes a clear demarcation between meekness, humility, gentleness, pride, selfishness, self-will, and arrogance.

> Enter into the heart of God's power

The character full of meekness is one who has been endowed with all that God is, one who has been led into the sacred inner chamber of God, who has spoken face to face, mouth-to-mouth with God and burnt by the fiery coal of the seraphic fire, fueled by the flame of the song, carried upon the sound of cherubic choir, branded by the red-hot finger of God's flashing lightning, whose eyes have been penetrated by the God who is consuming fire. Those who have been called to meekness are called to uncommon power. In a sense, the meekness of the powerless, to those delinquent in insight and power is the result of weakness and is pathetic.

To be truly meek a person must enter into the heart of God's power, plunge into the sacred mystery of Divinity and be enveloped in its terrifying power. Wherefore, when such a one speaks of meekness, we know that he has within himself/herself what might tempt him/her away from it. Meekness is then not a possession of people in themselves. It is the result of a choice and deliberate stance in the face of the possibility of self-overestimation and extension beyond the boundaries set by God. It comes because one is placed in a certain relationship with God and others and oneself, because one is where one is and who one is by virtue of what has been committed to one. It would seem then that since one is responsible for the privileged allowance that God has made for one, such a one then is called to choose to be meek. Here arises an understanding that though one has been placed in a particular situation because of one's access to Divine and human secrets, one must avoid being intractable in the use of the power that comes from that allowance or access.

Meekness in this sense speaks to one's stance as it concerns and contributes to the uplifting of others. Unless one knows the enormity of that which has been committed to them through that access and allowance into the power of the Divine and humanity, there can be no authentic stance of meekness. Meekness is thus meaningful as it causes the person to experience others in such a way that one allows the belonging (which has become one's by the unique Divine privilege) to draw others truly into the same belonging experience.

Meekness is a way of seeing God, the world, others and oneself. Meekness entails an understanding and acceptance of one's limitation even in the midst of power. Not the limitation of one's present condition but the limitation of one's power no matter how vast it may seem. This grasping of limitation and boundaries has a Divine potency, for it is in grasping this and being grasped by it that we make ourselves available to the Divine power inherent in the very idea of meekness. When seen as a response to human limitation, it causes whatever presumed power one may have to recede to the background as one submits to the empowerment of others who may lack what one has. Thus, it is the reference point and standard for being used by God and entering to the creative energetic movement that God is.

Experiencing Meekness

Meekness, as with other principles laid out in the Beatitudes by Jesus is a choice to be totally committed by our whole being as a way of realizing what is available beyond ourselves and in others. At this point the question may arise, "what are the ways of speaking and experiencing meekness?"

There is a surrendering aspect to meekness. Such surrender or commitment is founded upon the willingness to trust the greater, whose mere presence presents a limit to the one who must be meek. In order to understand meekness, we must endeavor to remove the rhetoric of victimization from the intention of the phrase "blessed are the meek". Thus, it must not be seen as "blessed are the victimized". In the meekness which Christ teaches, we posture ourselves in ways that accept the volatility of God's power and the necessity of holding it legitimately and openly without betraying it by arrogance — the arrogance of our sentimental partiality. There is a tension between meekness and power for those in whose lives it is evident. In those who have mastered it, meekness stands in tension with judgment.

Is meekness a moral concept? It is a posture based on choice. It is not that one knows him/herself as being meek, but one is positioned in the consciousness of others as being meek. Meekness arises out of a certain kind of self-awareness, and a certain kind of confidence in which one refuses to fray the boundaries which God has placed on those upon whom God has imbued power.

What is the person of the meek like in daily life? In daily interaction, what is the practical outflow of this way of being in the world? Let's look at the man Moses of whom it was said "*Moses was very meek, above all men on face the face of the Earth.*" (Numbers 12:3 KJV). Here is man, a man who, in the presence of God's power, understood his limitation but was also endowed with the power of God that could devastate and bring an empire to its knees. With a word he could make kings tremble with knocking knees. At the raising of his shepherd staff, he could tear the veil of nature and summon Earth's most tormenting pests to harass a kingdom of oppressors. His life was filled with a terrible and devastating force that could, in an instant, close the face of the Sun and at his word and the Earth open up its mouth and drink up men's life. He could call up an army of locust at whim. By simple word he could inundate the whole land with pesky flies. Yet this man with such immense power is called "the meekest man in all the Earth." What power was available to this man? How restrained he must have been in the use of that power. The world no longer knows meek men or women, those who have at their disposal unprecedented power and, without external pressure, are still able to restrain and resist the use of it for their own self-advancement.

> Meekness derives from true inner knowledge

Meekness is the internal restraint in the use of power for our own show, even though it is obvious that we have it. It is a restraint in power that is the result of authentic self-reflection and deep consideration of the impact of one's power on the world. Meekness, as it relates to Christ's teaching, entails a refutation of the false deification of force in which man disappears into the imposed image of the unconstrained nature or his artificially fabricated self. Meekness is also an acceptance of the finite, both in terms of the extent of our power and the longevity of our own lives.

The meek, with whatever power they have, take a leap of faith into the hand of God. Thus, as it relates to God, meekness is an affirmation of God's goodness and an acceptance of the sovereign protection and providence of God for those who trust in Him. There is a stance in which meekness entails an acceptance of suffering, but not torture nor injustice. Our Lord Jesus Christ speaking in Matthew 11:29 says, "*I am meek and lowly in heart.*" Jesus displayed meekness during the temptation. His whole interaction with the tempter was based squarely on the limitation which God has placed on man whose being he had taken upon himself. Though he had the power of God fully at his disposal, the limitation which God had placed on nature, man and the devil must be respected and be abrogated at will. So, he must maintain the tension which now must exist in those to whom God has given great power between self-immanence and self-transcendence.

A Fruit of the Spirit

Meekness calls forth the authentic mode of being. In Galatians 5:22-23, meekness is one of the Fruits of the Spirit. The life of the Spirit describes a life of quality which manifests God's ideal mode in our daily human interaction. Meekness is then one of the key measures for being led by the Spirit. It is one of the fruits or proofs of our walking in the Spirit. The best way to know if one is walking in the Spirit is to watch the level of their boastful use of power. If the opposite of meekness is pride then we can say that meekness is one way to avoid self-destruction. *"Pride goes before destruction, And a haughty spirit before stumbling. It is better to be humble in spirit with the lowly than to divide the spoil with the proud."* (Proverbs 16:18-19).

This is one the keys to joyful living, for it allows the continuous inflow of the Spirit. This is such a key that many great men and women of the Bible used to avoid falling headlong into destruction. Every person who was used effectively by God displayed this character. Such quality of person shows meekness in the constitution of the sphere of power. The one whose being is saturated by meekness knows himself and his God in an active and responsible way.

The Power to Transform the World

Meekness derives from true inner knowledge of the naked soul, which is the soul stripped of all its façade and false trappings. The meek, of their own accord, question their own self-confidence without losing their assurance, and question their power in order to redirect it into alignment with the purposes of God — but not in order to become so powerless as to lose their inner capacity to withstand the demonic. Rather, they become powerless in the sense of not using their power in the "normal" human way. Jesus, who was God, became powerless — but in this powerlessness was the power to transform the world. Thus, meekness is powerlessness in which the powerful are weakened, brute force becomes impotent and the rock calcified heart gives in to the gently flowing stream of God's mercy.

In essence, this means that what we perceive as meekness needs to be rethought. The structure of meekness has to begin with the landscape of what the meek person knows about himself and how that subjective self-awareness impacts various characteristics. How they appear to themselves, how God appears to them and how they appear to others. Various categories of meekness help to construct personal communal relationships. Meekness, as I have noted, does not exist where there is no consciousness of an opportunity for expression of power. Timid acquiescence to power out of weakness is not power. This is the type of definition that needs to be jettisoned. If meekness means anything, it is the result of enlightened insight into the profound Divine power that one carries.

Dimensions of Freedom

There is a noetic-thinking dimension to meekness which implies freedom.

A truth (aletheic) dimension to meekness which implies self-examination.

A dynamic (dunamis) power dimension to meekness which calls forth self-control.

A (thelematic) WILL-ing dimension to meekness which implies choice.

A faith (Pisteuic) dimension to meekness which carries assurance in the justice of God outworking everything for the good of those who love God and are called according to God's purpose.

A hope (Elpisoic) dimension to meekness which anticipates transformation.

It is courage to affirm life when it is in one's power to deny it. This is not just a decision to place people in scales of importance but of seeing everything in relation to the being of God and a willingness to grant each one into the open door. The meek man knows how to say yes or no without losing sight of his standing under the raised sword of Divine judgment. Meekness is grounded in a will that sees itself in the continuous flow of becoming. It knows that it has not arrived. This "not-yet-arrived" allows the meek to show mercy and grace. Meekness also needs to be viewed against human temporality and the possibility of sin that stands ready to invade even the strongest and most righteous of us all.

Meekness is the end result or the processional result that proceeds out of the focused power of the soul that has learnt to overcome fear. The Bible, in speaking of fear, states several things which need to be considered as one looks into meekness. The meek man has overcome a natural fear of God. Fear not in the sense of reverence but in terms of morbid terror which paralyzes impetus to action. The meek man has no fear of human beings. Having awakened to fear and considered it in the light of eternity, this man has ceased to fear what time may throw his way. In place of fear, he has established love. In place of fear, he has established assurance and is unshakable in the face of human power. The meek man walks in perfect love that has cast out fear. He is not caught any longer in the snare of man.

> *The fear of man brings a snare, but he who trusts in the Lord will be exalted.*
>
> Proverbs 29:25

He does not fear death, so he is willing to withhold the full expression of his own power so that others may stand in their Divinity if they so choose. If meekness is the result of having faced one's finite state and overcome the fear that comes with it, an awareness of eternity and seeing one's life in light of eternal reality, then meekness is closer to the God-nature than brute force and power. Banished from the inner psychic landscape of his/her life is helplessness in the face of the human condition. In his equanimity and poise, the meek one has directional intentionality which gives the capacity to make meaning out of meaninglessness. Such life is focused on God as the unshakable object of trust. The meek is never without an object on which to concentrate their energy and purpose. There is no need to direct their energy against others.

It is easy to deal with meekness as it relates to us and God but it is extremely difficult to deal with when we talk about it in relationship with human beings because it implies weakness in so many minds. When we see that meekness is a qualitative mode of being, deriving from the quality of heart relationship to God, then we become willing to accept and submit without resistance to the will and desires of God among the congregation of God. In dealing with one another, if meekness is the qualitative definition of our being, we overcome self-will and become more concerned about others than to focus on our own ways, ideas, and wishes. We are willing to put ourselves in second place and submit ourselves to achieve what is good for others. Paul says it this way *"For through the grace given to me I say to everyone among you not to think more highly of himself than he ought to think; but to think so as to have sound judgment, as God has allotted to each a measure of faith."* (Romans 12:3). Meekness is the opposite of self-will, self-interest, and self-assertiveness. Again, as I have noted, meekness is not a weakness but a strength. It is the inner strength to control one's power so that others can be free to manifest their destiny also.

Meekness as Making Space

Meekness, therefore, relates to God's posture of making room for the world. This making room for the realization of the destiny scrolls of others is intrinsic to the very nature of God and thus not a quality of mind whereby a person demeans themselves either by act or opinion. It is rather a clear and positive understanding of one's own goodness and value in the presence of God and the importance of acting as the expansive space in which others receive and realize their own value. To become a willing and dependable space in which Godly purposes for the world are born. Though there is an aspect of meekness which calls for submissiveness toward God, this submissiveness is a making ourselves available to be God's space for the ascension of others into God's teleology. In meekness, there is no self-righteous "I am better than that one" but rather an "I am willing to be the ground upon which they become better." Where there is not meekness, there is no space made for others or for God.

That there lack of meekness in our public discourse is obvious. For the religious and non-religious are constantly on the warpath to trip each other and to make sure that the other fails in the quest to help humanity. Rather than laying their lives as space for compassion without shame, each one wants to prove to us who can be the meanest. Meekness is diametrically opposed to much that goes on in our political confrontations. For the scriptures state: One who exalts self will be abased, one who puts self in the position of meekness will be exalted! (my paraphrase). We live a lie if we suppose that refusing to serve as space of expansiveness for the life of others, we preserve ourselves. We all deserve to be punished for our sins unless the meekness of Christ had served as a space for our reconciliation. Our hope of salvation is only by God's gracious provision of space in Himself for our forgiveness.

> one who puts self in the position of meekness will be exalted

Meekness and Contentment

Does meekness birth satisfaction and contentment or could it be that it is easier to flow in meekness when one's inner being is satisfied and content? The second part of the above question seems to be the case. When one has been confronted with life's exigencies and gone through the battle of life and death; when one has seen the terror of the abyss and emerged having received mercy from God, then arises this contentment. From this contentment flows a satisfaction which grows meekness. As such then, one is not easily moved by the trivialities and pettiness of this life plane, although one understands its sacredness. Such contentment does not arise from having all of one's desires met but by being at rest in the ultimate, which when desired is found completely by the rest of the soul in the spirit — in this case, union with God. Since meekness is power under control, then the idea of being content with who one is, one's knowledge of their place in God and in the universe becomes important. For most agitation and eagerness to prove oneself to others are mostly based on comparative pride and arrogance which arise out of discontentment, dissatisfaction and lack of assurance of one's place in the universe and God. Meekness, it seems to me, flows from satisfaction or contentment. Aristotle stated, "Happiness is self-contentedness." Meekness is self-contentedness, which bears fruits of happiness. Out of contentment flows a posture of praise to the LORD and a seeking of him from the depth of the heart. Thus, arises meekness.

Meekness then grows out of inner tranquility - the meek woman/man is not driven by the need of her/his own personal survival fundamentally since he/she has faced death and looked into the face of terror both inwardly and outwardly and is assured of her/his unshakable place in God and in the cosmos. Thus, the meek find tranquility in the face of insults, pain, denials, disappointments and death. Based on this tranquility the meek can stand for others, die for others and sacrifice for others and do so without bitterness and regret. When one understands himself/herself, one evaluates himself/herself not from the perspective of externality and others around them and what they say, rather they have an inner compass whose foundations cannot easily be stringed along by externality.

This awareness of one's place in the Divine and in the cosmos plays an important role in helping the meek attain their desired goals without losing sight of the ultimate purpose — union with the Divine. Meekness flows from the deep tranquility which has come as the result of the mastery of the demons of one's unconscious. The developed ability to access the Divine realities submerged in the subconscious chaos and order it for the positive and productive flow of relationship and self-restraint. This tranquility which comes from having confronted the depth of one's own being's abyss and the possibility of plunging into self-annihilation prompts one to act, not so much from self-preservation and self-protection, but from states of expansiveness and integration of being to be found only in one's rest in God. The life and acts of the meek come from contented, satisfied tranquility — not weighed down by the accumulation of false views of the self and negative experiences of the past. The meek finds rest in the wholeness of the Divine and attunement with the cosmos.

Now understand that meekness is not the result of positive emotions. It does not mean the maintenance of positive emotions at all times. Rather, it is the integrative synergy whose intentional synthesis or harmonization forms a bond of spiritual understanding and wisdom flowing into true justice and beauty.

Seek Meek

It seems that the meek insist on not letting irrationality engineered by culture, society and un-examined dogma detract from or create dissonance in their inner equilibrium and cause their ordered sphere of being to return to the chaos of the unorganized and inaccessible unconscious. At this juncture, it would seem appropriate to point out certain factors which uphold meekness and help the meek navigate their world.

1. The engagement of the deepest fears of the person before it can show itself. Moses had to delve into his deepest fear hidden in his psyche and the terror of God before he could display the meekness of which he is now so well known.

2. Learn to restrain in the process of dealing with opposition to one's inherent power.

3. Understand that unless one has reached the place of contentment, tranquility and satisfaction one may not have arrived at the place of meekness.

4. That there must be an expansive space within oneself

which is prepared for others to operate and manifest their self-realization and destiny.

The entire thrust of meekness is in the direction of being free from the lifeless and chaotic exertion of power which diminishes one's capacity to manifest God on Earth. One develops methods for thwarting and annulling the taunts of the enemy and goading to misuse their godlike power to demean other human beings and creation for the ascendancy of their sole individuality. It is then in meekness that we are able to develop characters and sensibilities and a variety of experiences which might simply be ruled out by the ungodly as being a weakness. In the sight of God, the righteous is salt that preserves and transforms. In truth, they enhance the Divine process in the world.

> meekness is the elevation of human life

Endurance, resourcefulness, ingenuity and discipline, control of anger and restraint of vengefulness are the marks of the meek. This it seems makes them inheritors of the Earth, as the Earth in its fragility and beauteous evolution and circular movement from life to death and death to life needs this gift of meekness to maintain its equilibrium. The power of this equilibrate principle is to be found in the heart of the meek.

Sons Of Your Father

This combination of contentment and tranquility which births meekness offers a blueprint for those who would understand God's dealing with the world, especially the Earth and its inhabitants. The meek have, it seems, accessed the pattern of the Divine perfection of which Jesus speaks when he said;

> "... that you may be sons of your Father who is in heaven; for He causes His sun to rise on the evil and the good, and sends rain on the righteous and the unrighteous. For if you love those who love you, what reward do you have? Do not even the tax collectors do

> *the same? If you greet only your brothers, what more are you doing than others? Do not even the Gentiles do the same? Therefore you are to be perfect, as your heavenly Father is perfect."*
>
> Matthew 4:45-48

There is within them the capacity to deal with a wide range of values and coordinate divergent settings so as to allow for the flow of the Spirit. Furthermore, the peculiarity of the meek in relation to most of their fellow human beings allows them to take in the real world as an intelligent spy who observes the subtle and salient patterns, collecting evidence to coalesce them into a coherent spiritual force within whatever ecological milieu they may find themselves. Thus, meekness is not a mere theoretical and abstract mode of being spiritual but rather, it is the elevation of human life above the animalistic by engaging the following of energetic systems and processes of God.

There is a keen understanding of the human journey and the nature of its incompleteness which allows the meek to give space to others, even when the weaknesses of others are obvious. As a result of this, the meek ones make great intercessors for the world. They are indeed the inheritors of the Earth. This capacity to maintain the Kingdom of Heaven on Earth by sheer openness to the Divine in others is a hallmark of their inter-relationship with others. They know in a sense that radical evil finds its gateway and definite flow from within and through the heart of man. So, they guard their heart and keep it focused on the preservation of the Divine destiny of others.

Here is not understanding of meekness apart from the movement of power and intention. Meekness is a culmination of the capacity for rulership ruling upon the Earth's realm. The culmination for Earthly rule — dominion spirituality. This idea is opposed to the limits set on the development of human spirituality as relating to self-realization by those who will control humanity. It accesses and exploits the inner riches of Divinity, encourages and nurtures itself to become trans-figurative, trans-mutative and transformative.

This moves beyond philosophizing and speculative generosity that bears no immediate fruit, to an engaged relevancy in the human condition which lifts it to its Divine destiny — to be like God.

After the elimination of that deeply ingrained vengeful pride, one enters into union and cooperation with the Spirit's impulse toward human self-realization. One has become meek. The plain truth is that the meek have understood that the realization of their selves in meekness is the realization of humanity in its destined communality. The life of the meek continuously draws the life in all they touch into the Divine matrix and invigorates with the Divine life.

Communal realization of the Divine seems to call for the continuous infusion of the spirit of meekness upon the land. The life of the meek is the lifeblood of the community's fulfillment of the Divine destiny. Such movement of the community through meekness comes through a transformation of character under the influence of beauty (harmony) — a state of contemplation which encourages the operation of grace and mercy. The question arises how far will meekness go for those who are being oppressed and to rid the world of pain caused by the misuse of power. How far will the meek go to encourage peace? It seems that inherent in the very process of being meek is the refusal to accept the inevitability of suffering caused by wanton misuse of power by humanity and to plunge oneself headlong into the possibility of the redemption of others even when they are unconnected to us. Oh, meekness!

The Meek Shall Inherit the Earth

> *The meek shall eat and be satisfied: they shall praise the Lord that seek him: your heart shall live forever.*
>
> *All the ends of the world shall remember and turn*

unto the Lord: and all the kindred of the nations shall worship before thee.

For the kingdom is the Lord's: and he is the governor among the nations.

All they that be fat upon earth shall eat and worship: all they that go down to the dust shall bow before him: and none can keep alive his own soul.

A seed shall serve him; it shall be accounted to the Lord for a generation.

They shall come and shall declare his righteousness unto a people that shall be born, that he hath done this.

Psalm 22:26-31 KJV

One meek one is accounted to the Lord as a thousand generations. They come in humble garb often ignored by a world that believes the louder, more obnoxious and arrogant one is the more they are to be honored - but it is the meek that shall declare the righteousness of the Lord to the generations to come. Inheriting the Earth is not the result of who is loudest or who strives to gather as much of its fleeting and illusionary wealth which flickers and dissolves into dust and flies away even while still in the process of being acquired.

So, what is the significance of the Earth? The Earth is not just a ball of mud, but is in itself an interwoven basket of seed forms that can be tended and used to penetrate the somatic psychic and pneumatic ecologies of creation in general. The Earth can be considered a Divine garden to be tended by the meek. It can also be seen as a seed to be nurtured to its fullness.

4TH BEATITUDE

4th Beatitude, Living a Satisfied Life: Blessed are those who hunger

**Blessed are those who hunger
and thirst for righteousness,
for they shall be satisfied.**

Matthew 5:6 6

Hunger is the need to eat, the desire for nourishment. Not many among those who are reading this work have been on the verge of starvation.

Hunger and lack of food leading to sickness or death is one of the worst kinds of death any human being can face on this plane of existence. In the last few years, we have seen what hunger can do. We have seen children dying because of hunger.

The medical dictionary offers three connotative possibilities of hunger;

1. a craving, desire, or urgent need for food;

2. an uneasy sensation occasioned normally by the lack of food and resulting directly from stimulation of the sensory nerves of the stomach by the contraction and churning movement of the empty stomach.

Definition "2" is more consequence of unattended hunger than a definition of what it is. Real hunger can lead to a weakened disordered condition, disease or even death. To die of hunger is one the most horrible deaths that one can watch. In true hunger, the body turns upon itself and feeds upon itself till all the muscles and tissues of the body are gone. The observer sees all but the skeletal remains, the semblance of the human that used to be. This is not what one may attach to blessedness!

Blessed Hunger?

The use of the "blessedness of hunger" is so radically jarring that one would think that Jesus was being sadistic - but far be it from the Master! The goal is to cause us to grasp the desperation with which we must seek, pursue, follow after and engage the LORD. Hunger and thirst denote a craving for life's sustaining nutrients. Unless there is this great need or desperate desire for righteousness, we remain dry. If care is not taken, we actually may die of self-cannibalization.

One can truly starve for lack of righteousness. If we are true to ourselves, we would agree that there is shortage of righteousness in our world today. Actually, there seems to be a quantum leap of the hunger for unrighteousness. This generation suffers from malnutrition, stemming not for lack of Divine food, but from the inability to be hungry and to be thirsty — the loss of appetite for righteousness. Hunger deprivation is worse than famine because there is food but the person is not hungry or does not realize that they are hungry until their body starves itself to death. It may also be that the spiritual stomach is filled with junk food, so that while the person is filled, they are filled with poison which seemingly nurtures the body but kills it in the process.

> every satisfaction brings into being a greater craving

True hunger comes from the emptiness inside. The problem with righteousness is that its arousal is not instinctual — it must be deliberate arising from an intentionality. We do not go looking for this hunger and thirst as our natural tendency, for it can only arise when we have tasted God within our spiritual being. It can be aroused by crises of consciousness. In those who do not know God, this hunger reveals itself as a lustful craving for fleshly fulfillment. However, this ravenous desire for God can only be real in the heart and soul of one who has tasted and seen that the Lord is good. This desire, this inner need, this passion yearning and longing for righteousness does not and can not result in gluttony but in satisfaction and rest for the soul. However, every satisfaction brings into being a greater craving and yearning for a deeper experience.

Hunger and thirst are fundamentally essential to the continued survival of human beings. It is not an evil thing to be hungry or thirsty, but to lack the capacity to satisfy is a great evil. The hunger and thirst of the human body is great but greater still is the soul's hunger and thirst. A most bitter plight indeed when its hunger and thirst for God is not satisfied. Many have been compelled to utter curses and to live in pathetic condition because their hunger for bread has not been satisfied. With mouth and tongue many hungry people around the world have called out in prayer for favor but it seems that they have been forgotten. Yet many go about without the hunger for righteousness or the thirst for it. Their spirit and the soul are starving to death, but they do not know it.

When Jesus says, "For what does it profit a man to gain the whole world and forfeit his soul?", (Mark 8:36). He speaks to the hunger for the things which cannot satisfy the soul, but rather depletes its energy and productivity.

Hunger for excellence and thirst for goodness, according to this Beatitude, cannot be denied. The Beatitude suggests that since God loves righteousness, the one who conceives righteousness in their mind will be satisfied with it. This hunger derives from the recesses of the heart and is answerable by God alone who has the power to see those things which are invisible given to created beings. There is in the most secret depth of man's being a Divinely created hunger and thirst, indubitably calligraphed in the incorruptible word. This experience of this necessary but contrary thing is regarded by Jesus to be a key to blessedness. Those who hunger do not consider themselves blessed but rather feel justified in their accusation against God and Society.

Seldom does one go about blessing, and praising God for hunger. But this hunger is not a physical lust for material satisfaction but a heart-seeking, engaged, relational intimacy with the existential underpinning which is God. This hunger and thirst is symbolic of the inner processes of our soul which, in the first instance, cannot find its bearing on account of our innate sinfulness, until the spirit of God comes to dwell within us.

Hunger and thirst are gifts from God. To hunger and thirst may be painful but not to hunger and not to thirst is a curse to be avoided.

The Object of the Hunger and the Thirst

Jesus puts righteousness as the object of the hungry and thirsty in this passage. How can people hunger and thirst for righteousness if they are dead in their trespasses? It will seem that this Beatitude is directed to those who have tasted righteousness. That is, until we are born of the Spirit and of water, we have not experienced righteousness. When righteousness is truly hungered and thirsted for, there is a download of blessings. They shall be filled! When the hunger for righteousness causes us to make God's righteousness the most important priority, everything about our fulfillment becomes God's priority. Righteousness is intimately connected to the Kingdom of God. It is interesting that Jesus does not say to seek first the Kingdom of Heaven, but seek first the Kingdom of God. Jesus said it this way, "Seek ye first the Kingdom of God and his righteousness and ALL these things shall be added unto you." (Matthew 6:33 KJV). Righteousness, in this sense of the inner, is the essential nature of God.

In man, righteousness is revealed as the willingness to believe what God says. As we read in Genesis 15:6 *"Then he believed in the Lord; and He reckoned it to him as righteousness"*. Furthermore, in many places in Scripture, righteousness is intricately connected with justice. Thus, it is not just what human beings believe about God, it is the fact that they believe God's word that God will do what God says. Again, when speaking about Abraham God says in Genesis 18:19, *"For I have chosen him, so that he may command his children and his household after him to keep the way of the Lord by doing righteousness and justice, so that the Lord may bring upon Abraham what He has spoken about him."*

The two pillars upon the genetic Divinity of the children of Abraham will stand for all eternity are righteousness and justice. The book of Amos speaks of it as two streams intertwining with each other; *"But let justice roll down like waters And righteousness like an ever-flowing stream."* (Amos 5:24). These are two pillars that hold up the throne of the everlasting God; *"So the Lord commanded us to observe all these statutes, to fear the Lord our God for our good always and for our survival, as it is today. It will be righteousness for us if we are careful to observe all this commandment before the Lord our God, just as He commanded us."* (Deuteronomy 6:24-25)

> *Righteousness and justice are the foundation of Your throne; Loving kindness and truth go before You. How blessed are the people who know the joyful sound!*

O Lord, they walk in the light of Your countenance. In Your name, they rejoice all the day, And by Your righteousness they are exalted. For You are the glory of their strength, And by Your favor our horn is exalted. For our shield belongs to the Lord, And our king to the Holy One of Israel. Once You spoke in vision to Your godly ones, And said, "I have given help to one who is mighty; I have exalted one chosen from the people.

Psalm 89:14-19

> God will not be silent to the heart that cries for righteousness

God will not be silent to the heart that cries for righteousness. No portion of what naturally or spiritually belongs to such a one shall be left at the altar for the evil one to feast upon. One cannot be hungry or thirsty objectively - it is an experience that requires the participation of the whole person. It is this hunger for God that led Abraham to leave father, mother, family, clan and country for God, thus engendering the promise, *"In your seed all the nations of the earth shall be blessed because you have obeyed My voice."*

This satisfaction of which Jesus speaks happens at various levels of the hungering and thirsting person. This Beatitude carries with it a promise exceedingly full for the mind of those who freely choose to make this hunger and thirst the mark of their existence. The seeking of righteousness cannot be done without seeking the Kingdom of God. Whenever righteousness is sought without the Kingdom of God it becomes self-righteous and arrogant. However, when our hunger and thirst for righteousness are Kingdom-oriented there comes with it freedom from curse, disease, and defeat from the enemy. Hungering and thirsting for righteousness, for those who understand it, exerts all the panoply of feelings and passion which affects the seeker at all levels of his being. The power of such a state of desire is that it comes with the possibility of sound health. Our powers of seeing, hearing and acting, all those which belong to the outward senses, our appetites which are conversant about pleasures are placed at our soul's disposal to use in its quest to be filled with the righteousness of God and His Kingdom. Every other thing is reduced to nothing. Our only agitation is to find the righteousness and be filled to fullness by it — and there, true tranquility.

It is interesting that the Lord uses two cravings to speak of in this Beatitude — to receive the full blessedness of this Beatitude and enjoy the great happiness and prosperity resulting from a satisfied content life. Hungering alone will not do, there must accompany also the thirst for the water of the word.

> *"Behold, days are coming," declares the Lord God, "When I will send a famine on the land, Not a famine for bread or a thirst for water, But rather for hearing the words of the Lord."*
>
> Amos 8:11

All These Things

'Hunger and thirst for righteousness' have several things wrapped up in its sphere. It is the desire for prudence, understanding, knowledge and wisdom. The one who hungers for righteousness, hungers for the body of God as his or her only food. God also gives him irresistible power. For the kingdom of God is *"righteousness, peace and joy"* and to seek *"first the kingdom of God"* adds *"all these things."* Hunger and thirst are instruments for calling for the harmony of the dimensions of God's infinite supply into one's life. It is that vessel or bowl which is able to contain the fullness of God in it. It is *"all these things"*.

Hungering and thirsting for righteousness is a hunger for the ability to keep God's rules regulations and laws. It is to have an ardent desire for God as God — not God as some sideshow or appendix to one's life which can either be dealt with or not depending on whether one needs him materially or not. If it is true that the righteous man is the "prop of all the human race" then, by this hungering and thirsting, one is seeking to bring to manifestation God's being in all of creation. He is deeply seeking for God to bestow God's self as a treasure to every human soul.

The truth about righteousness is that whoever seeks it needs not to seek for any other thing and chase after secondary matters. Whoever finds it has found the end of all searches, and he that gets it does not get it just for himself but for all humanity. The thing about righteousness is that you cannot find it without becoming it. When found, it brings with it all wealth and the full bounty of God - it brings God unhindered and unencumbered. If you desire God to open up the treasures of Heaven and pour showers down upon you of all kinds of good things together in such a way that all the channels on Earth are filled with them to overflowing, then you must pray for this hunger and thirst for righteousness. Those who have this hunger genuinely are never rejected. Their prayers are prayed from the center of Divinity and saturated with God himself. They are not addressed to God as an object, for they are not "another" to God, but instead are "in" his image and likeness, for they continually operate within the force of His will.

It is the spark of favor, the expressive equivalency, the good, the fertilization of the Earth, the unmediated experience of the goodness of God in all things. Where righteousness is present, though all things are destroyed, by its fragrance and virtue, life is reborn. By a spark of fire, the world can be set ablaze even when it has been covered by a long, dark, frigid winter. By the attainment and filling of this righteousness even the dead can be raised and the fallen can be quickened to stand. Even the extinct can be a called back to existence. Why? Because righteousness is God in God's very essence. Blessed are those who hunger and thirst for righteousness for they shall be filled!

Benefits of Righteousness

> *The righteous man will flourish like the palm tree, He will grow like a cedar in Lebanon. Planted in the house of the Lord, They will flourish in the courts of our God. They will still yield fruit in old age; They shall be full of sap and very green, To declare that the Lord is upright;*

He is my rock, and there is no unrighteousness in Him.
Psalm 92:12-15

The one who has been given the gift of hungering and thirsting after God's righteousness, and has been filled or satisfied in mind and soul, is like a pillar in the house of God. Having found satisfaction for their hunger and thirst, they are firmly established as points of contact for the relief and healing of humanity. This relief which comes from being filled results in Divine health and peace of mind. But to get here one must abandon all satisfaction which comes from the ego and from worldly sources. One must be completely consumed through and through by a clear vision of intimacy with God. When such a one worships, they employ their whole being and cast it before the Lord as the sick cast their whole being in the care of their physician. This being filled, this being satisfied is like spreading, "salve over the wounds of the soul, which folly, and injustice, and all the other multitude of vices, being sharpened up, have grievously inflicted upon it." (Philo Judaeus of Alexandria).

Those who do not hunger and thirst after righteousness are often swallowed spirit, soul and body by a great stormy deluge of restlessness. However, those who are satisfied are invigorated and empowered to overstep the stormy waves, riding on their surface as Jesus did. They rise above the dangers which threaten, with God being at the center of their satisfaction, they often escape in safety. They are like a tree that bears fruits of knowledge, understanding and wisdom. The bearing of useful fruit grows out of Divine satisfaction. Righteousness is the roots of true goodness, though in the world in which we live it may seem that it is often obscured by the ascendancy of those who appear to flourish in wickedness. Yet, in the Divinely appointed time, God will bring its fruit to light.

Those who hunger and thirst after righteousness receive the garments which are called "praise" because it is woven of the three supernatural threads which are called Wisdom, Knowledge, and Understanding. These bring forth the spirit of sonship and cause the child of God to flourish — not only in specific seasons and times but allows one to operate from the eternal dimension which has its roots beyond mere chronological time. The Bible states clearly that *"Abraham believed God and it was counted to him for righteousness"*. When God says to Abraham *"I will surely return to you at this time next year; and behold, Sarah your wife will have a son."* (Genesis 18:10). Sarah must be made hungry and thirsty for the realms of eternity. She and Abraham entered the Heavenly realm of the eternal Eden from where comes the two "HEH" (ה) which are now inserted into their destiny and from there draw down the life that comes from the future times of the Messiah. Abraham must combine wisdom and understanding in order to birth knowledge of God upon the face of the Earth. For Isaac represents for us the flow of sonship knowledge into the realms of creation. It is the combination of the three, which brings forth a son, who represents knowledge.

"For the earth will be filled with the knowledge of the glory of the Lord, As the waters cover the sea." (Habakkuk 2:14). A hunger and thirst for righteousness is the stirring of the Heavens by the desire of the righteous to see the glory. That is, to see Shekinah poured forth without reservation upon all flesh, who will then release it into all the dimensions from which human beings were formed. The threefold cord of Wisdom, Understanding and Knowledge causes the believer to be filled with righteousness. Those whose singular desire is to be the medium for the flow of the glory of God from the supernatural to the creation below. The eternal makes His passage into creation and all is rectified. They shall see God.

> We pursue intimacy with God

A hunger and thirst for righteousness implies a desire to be before the throne of God and commune with Him in the deepest of places. It is not mere obedience to the letter of the law but a passionate longing for intimacy. It is a bending to the Lord and a pressing pursuit that consumes one with the consuming fire that is the Lord wherever he may lead. To be consumed by a consummation that leaves us whole and more human and more Divine. The hunger and thirst in the heart of Abraham is what led him to obey the Lord's commandment. He went there not just to inherit a piece of land but to find a place where he could be fed from the supernatural realm and the river from the crystal sea. Abraham's hunger for

God, in the end, is celebrated among angels and men. When we, with all our soul, body and mind, thirst for that righteous stream which flows from virtuous Eden, we are able to tread with Divine steps on the head of the serpent, crushing every lust with a righteous hunger and thirst for the waters from the fountain of life. We pursue intimacy with God at all times and in all places, pressing our face through the veil to worship and cry thrice "Holy" and twice "Abba." The hungering and thirsting through every Divine silence is a consuming hunger. Every moment of silence stirs a thirst - as the deer pants for the waters.

Eternal separation.

The summation of the beautiful and praiseworthy is in eating from the incandescent bread that is His body, a drinking from the crystal-clear fountain that is His life. This is the posture and manner of being for those who hunger and thirst for the righteousness that is the person of the LORD. This is the one act of their spirit, soul and body — it's unifying principle and purpose, his/her guiding light in the path of his/her life. Herein lies one of the basis for the blamelessness which is often attributed to weak and frail women and men. Here is what makes a saint — not the attainment of perfect acts or the attainment of wise action in every detail of life. For we can always look and find cracks of fear, unbelief, and even some weaknesses of which we may decry, but we may be looking at the wrong place. For the respect which God and the angels and saints may look, they hear instead the hunger and thirst. It is in the hungering and thirsting heart that God looks.

5TH BEATITUDE

5th Beatitude, What Goes around Comes around: Blessed are the merciful

Blessed are the merciful for they shall obtain mercy.
Matthew 5:7

The Greek word for mercy here is the word *eleeo* (ἐλεέω; el-eh-eh'-o). It connotes the willingness and capacity to help the afflicted who is in need and seeking aid. It is not just the feeling of pity but the active engagement of the whole person to help the afflicted and the wretched condition of others.

When we experience mercy from God, it is not God feeling sorry for us but the engagement of the whole being of God into our active salvation. Mercy is an incarnational term. When we obtain mercy, we show mercy. We show God in the human condition. Mercy is a word that is all-inclusive. It is a term that combines in its root the masculine as the plural bearer of seed and the feminine as the one who gives birth to action. It is a word that can be used to describe the interior content of the human soul but can also describe the human act. In it lies the root of compassion. One can be merciful as well as do mercy. When it is drawn out in terms of pity without action, it can lead to the disdain of the person in need - a patronizing debilitation of the recipient.

Bowels and Brains

Even the word *oikteírō* (οἰκτείρω), which may be called "visceral-compassions", grows out of mercy. One who has mercy as an innate nature, experiences deep shaking in their bowel which may lead to lamentation (as we find in the prophet Jeremiah). When we say that God has mercy or that God is merciful, we are looking at God metaphorically as a mother whose bosom trembles at the sight of the suffering of her child - whether the suffering is the result of the child's own doing or not. The ancients thought that bowels were the seat of compassion and the heart was the seat of will and thought. Both the heart and the bowels are connected together so that when bowels are moved by mercy the heart births forth compassion.

If we look to the Hebraic background of this concept of mercy and compassion, notice that there are several words which are translated mercy. One of the words translated mercy is the Hebrew word *racham* (רַחֲמִים) — which often appears in the plural denoting its inclusion of the emotions, deep longings of the soul for the welfare of another and activities deriving from the feeling of pity for another human being. This word comes from the root "*rakham*", which literally translates womb or bowels — as used in 2 Chronicles 30:9 "*For if you return to the Lord, your brothers and your sons will find compassion before those who led them captive* and will return to this land. For the Lord your God is gracious and compassionate, and will not turn His face away from you if you return to Him," and I Kings 8:50 "and forgive Your people who have sinned against You and all their transgressions which they have transgressed against You, and make them objects of compassion before those who have taken them captive, that they may have compassion on them". To the Hebrew mind, the word compassion is intricately woven with the idea of mercy and the act of mercy.

So what is compassion? It can also connote to sympathy, which means simply to have the same pathos / feeling as another synchronically. To have it in the midst of their experiencing that pathos sadness, and not after. To have sympathy after is regret and cannot lead to actions that alleviate suffering, but mainly to apology. To have it synchronously with another may lead to immediate action meant to relieve the pain. 'Merciful' is not merely an adjectival description of a person or thing, for it cannot be used merely as a noun but must be tied to the act of the person whom it describes. It must have an outward manifestation which moves the person beyond him/herself to become incarnated in the life of the one who needs the show of mercy. The Merciful person finds as the subject of his character his or her fellow human beings who impinge upon his bowel and causes it to tremble until prophetic action is birthed. The merciful person meets the needs of others and the one in need receives without lowering their humanity or losing their dignity. More than giving resources just to meet the need and prove his capacity for being merciful as a show, the merciful man or woman first gives of themselves as a gift to the other so that their inner man is realized in the humanization of the other.

> Mercy is a self-giving outflow

Mercy as One of the "Is-ness" of God

It is in this sense that God is said to be *"rich in mercy"* (Ephesians 2:4). It is from the being of God as *rak'hum* that salvation flows for all humanity who stand dejected in their abject poverty of righteousness — until God, in giving of His self, offers that Divine self as salvation. When the Bible says that God is merciful to those who fear him, it must be remembered again that God is called the 'Fear of Israel'. That awe, which is the nature of God, is what God gives when he shows mercy. Mercy is a self-giving outflow of the inner nature of the one who shows it. When God shows mercy, it is aimed at restoring the one who receives it, creating inner peace, rescuing their lost self-respect and God's glory experientially in the soul. Mercy is uplifting and restorative. Whenever the righteous shows mercy, they disarm the enemy's capacity for putting a human being to shame. By an act of mercy, guilt is driven away and a thanatic tendency (toward death) is put out and replaced with a desire and zest for life. Mercy gives the power to restore joy and dignity.

Mercy can also be seen as favoring the unfavorable. Its presence is indicative of the fact that the one showing mercy believes in the future hope and possibility of the receiver.

Another important fact to emphasize is that mercy implies love. Not love as intimacy with the one for whom mercy is shown but rather as love as a Divine mode of being. The process of mercy carries with it the seeds of creative transformation of the circumstance and the person within it. Mercy controls the vengeance-driven, animalistic tendency which has so often taken ascendancy over humanity in so many ways. The objective of mercy is to subject the self, ridden by this animalistic vengeance, to the self-influenced by the Holy Spirit of God. It presents the person with the opportunity to function in the image of God. Thus, every opportunity for mercy is a moment to subordinate our whole being to the likeness of God and our Divinity. It is in reality, the regulatory energetic system for balancing personal relationships. The primacy of mercy is seen in the way that God relates to the world. It is a dynamic principle whose manifestation depends on the interior strength of the person that calls it forth.

Mercy's significance may lie partly in the fact that it arises from the inner core of an individual. This means that it always triumphs over judgment. It is not possible that any situation could arise in this world, concrete or spiritual, in which mercy cannot assert its superiority.

Mercy is one of the few things that is considered eternally intrinsic to the nature of God. The stirring of much tension and conflicts within relationships, both personal and social, calls truly for the necessity of mercy as a fundamental mode of being in our day. Where the substrata of person and community lack mercy, it so easy to be threatened. Anxiety arising out of this lack of mercy at the foundation then enables man's worst expression of self-preservation. Mercy enables human beings to mature and evolve in an atmosphere which minimizes both inner and external conflicts. Matt Ferkany, in his essay 'Mercy As an Environmental Value', states that "What matters for susceptibility to mercy is that the recipient can be made better or worse off in some respect and that the agent of mercy has the power to make him better off in that respect. For these reasons it is best to say that the merciful person is motivated simply by recognition and concern for the good of the other, not necessarily compassion." (p4).

Mercy, in its essence, expresses the fact that it is possible to change certain human tendencies and to upgrade them by the distributive wave of the Spirit of God within the merciful. In this, the merciful shows he/she to be independent of the fatalism of the human condition and convention of his/her age. Thus, the expression of mercy is not the dilution of strength but a gradual flow of the elementary vibrations of the Divine that perpetually repeats itself and eternally flows into all of creation - as we read *"for His mercy endures forever."*

Mercy retards human degradation, for when the will raises mercy it raises the image of God in another. In doing so, it raises both the merciful and receiver to creative action which undoes the flow of pain and shame. Mercy is a vital activity whose movement turns around the human tendency to seek revenge. It causes the merciful to turn back to the true natural/Divine flow of man. A human, being in his/her fallen state, has a tendency to vengefulness, no doubt, and by compulsion lashes out in violent and destructive self-defense either inwardly or outwardly. When inwardly it turns the self against the self, when outwardly it turns the self against others.

Christ makes so much of our spiritual vitality dependent on our capacity to operate in mercy in our daily lives. We are also able to go through various psychic stages and cause pneumatic transmutation more quickly (and probably with a little more ease) if we are merciful. Mercy is in a sense a meditative mode of being which is able to help us re-establish the conditions necessary for tapping into the spiritual power made available for us when our relationship with the Lord is established. If you may, it is the modal connective combination of the elemental substances relating to each other in such a way that new creation realities emerge. By its in-gathering and self-unifying flow, it rebuilds the pathways of our mind and keeps us in emotional purity, so that when one looks at himself, what is mirrored back is the clarity of conscience which releases one into truth and freedom.

The Fulfillment of Purpose

Mercy is useful in cooperating with others for the fulfillment of purpose.

> enlightened by the love of God through mercy

The presence of mercy in us and from others, removes the disturbing pneumatic dissonance which can distort, disrupt, delay or even destroy our spiritual progress. So, mercy elicits in us reactions which are essential to positive self-alteration. Because mercy is called for in the context of disturbance or dissonance to the pneumatic/psychic equilibrium, it is seen as the harmonization of antagonistic conditions. Without mercy, the reaction may be far more intensive and complicated and sap the vitality of those involved. The ingenuity of being merciful in light of faith can also be considered in terms of how the presence of the flow for mercy can help restore us to spiritual malleability. For the impetus of mercy with the merciful move the giver to be open not only to friends but to "enemies."

The merciful see an image of God in the other. This image connects the center of their own being with that of another, so that they do not look at the other as floating unattached to their being. To be merciful, as seen in scripture, calls for an intentional preferentiality in which the person is attentive to the flow of the Divine between their own being and the person of another. Paul enjoins us to see the feeling of mercy or the act thereof from the perspective of the benefits which we have received from God and the universe. Such attentiveness is meant to awaken within us a flow of care and concern for those who do not deserve it because of the scars left by their action upon us.

This alteration in the vital spirit is operated from mercy as the intentional inducement of new vitality and expansion of one's inner consciousness of God. Mercy then serves as an energetic impulse for the miraculous. For mercy is tied at depth to compassion and opens the gate for the exchange of Divine creative force. Mercy should not be conceived as a second-order process which serves mainly to maintain order or defer pain. Rather, it can be seen as an instrument for integrating and inter-weaving the flow of the Divine nature into the everyday life. The law of mercy, if I may call it so, releases the potential for relational communicative action. The merciful gain a spiritual orientation toward understanding which gives them freedom from the instinctive bent toward mental, ideological or even physical violence. Often in life, as great demands and pressures are placed upon us, we tend toward overload and the boiling overflow of anger. The move toward understanding the other from their humanity, enlightened by the love of God through mercy, heightens compassion and empathy.

A Divine Attribute

Mercy is the only item of equal exchange with itself. Nothing can be exchanged equality with it that does not carry its DNA, other than itself. Mercy is at the heart of righteousness and holiness. The

Master ends this Beatitude by stating without equivocation that those who are merciful 'obtain' mercy. The use of the Greek word [Verb] *krateo* which means "to be strong," points to the fact that there is a power principle or an empowerment principle for the merciful within the act of mercy.

The very act of mercy propels one toward the capacity to gain possession of mercy. Mercy or the obtaining of mercy is a particular end purpose of life. If we take the combination of the term *krateo* and combined it with merciful *hilaskomai*, as used in profane Greek, we may come to the idea that being merciful empowers the merciful to be a conciliator, to be an appeaser in a context of offense, to be a propitiator for the offense of others against God and causing there to be reconciliation. Because the act of showing mercy is not natural to sinful humanity, especially when he/she is in the right, such goodwill or mercy orientation is the result of an intentional labor on the part of the one who shows it.

Mercy is not a natural reflex but an outflow of a disciplined compassionate response to offense. It requires work. This Beatitude by the Lord makes it appear that mercy, at a certain level, is something to be earned. So, while we do not merit mercy, we can sow ourselves into more of it by how we handle those who need mercy from us. This is unlike the pagan deities whose relationship with a human being tended more toward unmitigated fatalism, alienation and even antagonism. God of the Bible is shown having Mercy as an essential attribute of His being. Man, alienated not by his natural state but by his self-alienation through sin, yet by God's inherent tendency toward pity and compassion, the human being is always available and is to be birthed in mercy. He is "the Father of mercies," (2 Corinthians 1:3), ever ready to release this mercy to the undeserving. Because he is the "Father of mercies", whosoever shows mercy touches the depth of the being God and activates its flow through them and for them.

The ground upon which believers are sown into salvation is the ground of mercy under whose Law of Divine return they operate and live. When believers exhibit mercy one toward another, their hearts of compassion connect two places - both the world and the supernatural. The angelic within the material is released and empowered to manifest the grace and glory of the Godhead upon the world of creation. Every flow of compassion upon the Earth is preceded by a stirring of tender mercies in God above, which then reverberates in the heart of the righteous below. Most believers know that it is by the flow of mercy that conciliation with God is possible. There is a connection made by Jesus between humility and the flow of mercy. The humble heart is a vessel for receiving mercy. That is not to say that mercy is only shown to the humble. This mercy, indeed is given to all, poured out like water from the heart of the Father of Lights, as signified by the emphasis of scripture as the deeply flowing and swift river rising from the Eden of God's love.

Be Like God

> *But the tax collector, standing some distance away, was even unwilling to lift up his eyes to heaven, but was beating his breast, saying, 'God, be merciful to me, the sinner!' I tell you, this man went to his house justified rather than the other; for everyone who exalts himself will be humbled, but he who humbles himself will be exalted.*
>
> Luke 18:13

The prayer of the tax collector, and declaration of the Lord that he went to his house justified, shows God's desire to be propitious, merciful, compassionate and easily placated. He is waiting for a heart that can receive and be intimately transformed by mercy's reception.

That God is not of Himself already alienated from man is clear from the fact that He is constantly seeking to be in relationship with man. We find this in His attitude of quick acceptance of the sinner who turns to him. The being of God charged with mercy moves toward the transmutation and transformation of the sinner, even with minimal effort on the part of the sinner. While God's holiness is intrinsic and God is pure in all ways, yet in mercy God provides sin expiation atonement and a flow of compassion which necessitates the acceptance of the sinner into God's holiness and space of Divine creativity. This again supports the fact that mercy is the clothing of and for His righteousness. This is the expiation force of mercy provided by God in the atoning sacrifice of His Son. For a man of mercy, though he be a sinner himself, God activates this force in His act of mercy. For in mercy, God commands and delivers cleansing to the one who has sinned against Him. In activating mercy and forgiveness, the receiver himself is laid length and breadth upon the flowing mercies of God. It is mercy that assuages Divine wrath, ameliorates hostility and presents an unshackled future from God to men. One of the most powerful ways to tap into what God has accomplished for us in Christ, by His death, and to release man into Divine becoming and regeneration, is not only to accept the mercy of God but to imitate that mercy which God himself has shown.

By Mercy and compassion we attain unto Divinity and our sonship begins to manifest. Obtaining Divinity and meeting within the inner sanctuary of the heart of God is set by riding upon the flashes of mercy and compassion. Mercy is a signifier and sign which "to obtain, allows our soul to reach beyond things and to translate what seems to be merely physical and crass materialism into the help that is from God's heart." For example, it is by mercy that the salvation which is in Christ Jesus, and the eternal glory that comes with it, is made possible. There can be no effective ministry without mercy, for it is mercy that obtained for us the possibility of ministry in the person of the Lord Jesus Christ. Mercy, let us reiterate, is not pity but compassionate in action where the merciful, through their priesthood, activates in the life of the other realities of the High priestly acts of Christ.

There are several ways to look at the obtainment of mercy as stated by the Lord. First, it is the receiving of mercy into one's own being, the one being forgiven. But in another way, it is the obtainment of the character of mercy in terms of being given the gift of Divinity to be like God. This obtainment of Divine resemblance shows that, in giving mercy, one finds within themselves the voice of God that sits in the center of their being. In so doing, they procure for themselves mercy. In mercy, one is accomplishing the telos (end goal), the fruit of maturation, which may have taken several years to reap in view of the natural process of maturation. In a sense, one is eating of the fruit of the tree of their maturation from the future in the present act of mercy.

Mercy is then connected to the redemption of time by accessing eternal redemption for the one to whom mercy is shown and for the one who shows mercy. There is a sense of a double extraction of the lost time for both parties involved in the act of mercy. How mercy seems to intensify and fortify the strength of the weak is well-known. Helping translate, transmute and translocate the persons involved in it is witnessed by what it has done for us from the side of God our Father. Mercy, when shown, is an immediate martyrdom, a *martureo* (bearing of witness), an insertion of Voice to those who have lost their voice.

> Mercy and compassion are instruments for securing the future

Mercy is *peripoiesis* (preserving / saving) work of making a wall defense around another to protect the vulnerable. This poetic saturation of the vulnerable, in that they are seen from the insight of their possibility rather than their immediate place of failure, is a way of helping the person into salvation in its completeness (in that it may help them acquire both the insight and strength to enter into their spiritual possession). This *peripoiesis*, this poetic of surrounding love, helps to preserve hope and meaning. By its gainful correspondence to the inner life of God, it witnesses the very mercy of God in the world.

The Choice of Mercy

Mercy is not a mere emotional reaction to the plight of another but rather it is a deliberate and thought through action that also demands a deliberate and willing reception of that mercy which is offered. The hand of mercy extended must be taken hold of and held onto so that the intent of the heart is transferred into the being of the one who receives and takes hold of it. Receiving or accepting mercy is a way of gaining access into the grace upon the life of other persons. In gaining this access, it is also giving access to someone as a visitor and is giving access to the house for succor. As we are in constant need of mercy, we ought also to show mercy frequently. For it is written that the God whom we call Father is *"quick to show mercy"*. It does not mean that we shirk the need for a sense of taking the responsibility for our errors and sins, or that we become secure in our inordinate undertakings, but rather by "the predominance mercy we strengthen the application of righteousness."

The Hebrew speaks of the mercies of Abraham and Messianic believers who speak of the mercies of our Lord Jesus Christ by which we assumed the responsibility of being those who keep alive the promises in the lives of our "undeserving" brethren. If the thought of mercy is used as a key to raising up of sons and bringing them to maturity, perhaps restoration will not be an alien thought to us who seek to walk in mystical union with the Lord. The first responsibility of such as seek to manifest the heart of the Father, surely will not be the destruction of the weak or the fallen but that of mercy restoring faith in "receiving" the promises of the Father.

If we attached any significance to the deep sense of God's compassion, we will indeed undertake to exercise mercy and move others in that mercy towards the fulfillment of the promises of God in their lives. In receiving mercy, one recovers the depth of gladness from the Divine, welcoming again into the context of humanity the inner ecstasy of the Godhead, giving the one who receives it the impetus toward metamorphosis. In giving mercy, one acknowledges inner Divinity. In accepting it, one acknowledges and draws into their being a repairing motion which they can then use to harmonize the world for others and for themselves.

The believer is laboring to make oneself a vessel of mercy which is not only a receptacle of mercy but is also a dispenser of mercy. Mercy and compassion are instruments for securing the future. No one can travel to the future and obtain its inheritance, who lacks mercy.

6TH BEATITUDE

6th Beatitude, Visional Clarity: Blessed are the pure in heart

**Blessed are the pure in heart,
for they shall see God.**

Matthew 5:8

In order to deal with this Beatitude, I want to ask a simple question. What does it mean to be pure? The first definition in the dictionary is "not mixed". Something whose natural chemical, color or look is not mixed with any other substance.

It is not 10% cotton, 20% linen, and 70% wool. If it is wool, it is 100%, hence it is pure wool. If it is cotton, it is 100% cotton. If it is Linen it is 100% linen. It is free from contamination and hence it is clean. Pure can also mean that something is complete, not missing any of its parts. It is whole, in that it is whole in its integral nature. When Jesus uses the word 'pure', he is speaking of a heart as relating to holiness, wholly separated unto God unadulterated and uncontaminated, unpolluted by the world. Jesus is not speaking of a sinless moral existence but of an integral whole in which all of one's being is committed to the pursuit of God and God's purpose. When Jesus speaks of the heart, we know that He is not speaking of the blood-pumping organ. He is speaking of the heart as the basis for moral, spiritual and emotional life. A pure heart entails outflow of the deepest and clearest transparency from a person's innermost recesses. In relationship with God, one allows themselves vulnerability as God allows access to His self, even to the pain that can be caused by outgoing love. This inner, unsullied, outreaching love then flows into one's habit and character. Part of the realization of this purity of heart is in compassion, which is an empathetic ability for affection, love, and grace — even in the most adverse conditions.

The Heart Cannot Be Hidden

There is a thread that runs through the whole biblical literature. It is required of prophets, seers, judges, kings and the common man on the street who wants to relate with God at the level of deeper intimacy. Those who develop 'purity of heart' are the ones who have truly lasting and great power in matters of spirituality. It is needed in the busy work-a-day world in which we live. It cannot be compromised without one exchanging or trading and battering away some vital part of one's destiny for a period of time. Until a pure heart is sought for and returned in some form, Divinely ordained goals are thwarted, visions are darkened to a lesser or larger degree and success is tainted

> In the pure heart springs thought

with a streak of darkness. By it, a person can build a working fluid motion, a matrix of weaved life in which temporality is in constant manifest interaction with eternity at a complex level. Heart purity is a force that can buttress, enliven and make a human motion toward an unstoppable vision. The purity of heart shapes our life and gives our life vigor of spirit. It determines our attitude, altitude, and relational impetus. The purity of heart affects our aesthetic orientation and health. The state of the mind and thought reflects the content of the heart. The purity of heart births beauty and goodness. Jesus tells us that "*out of the abundance of the heart the mouth speaks.*" Whether we like it or not, the content of our heart cannot be hidden too long before it is forced to the fore.

Heart purity, like the natural healthy heart, refines and purifies our out flowing character, attitudes, habits and sentiments. A pure heart is needed to attract purity, beauty, wonder, harmonious interaction with creation. To the degree that one has a pure heart, there is released a subtle power capable of restructuring even the hardest veil separating one from the greater spiritual dimensions for which one is destined. In the pure heart springs thought, ideas visions and imaginations that affect the world at its most basic level. Purity is a heart in quest of the holiness of God.

Whoever thinks he can experience the fullness of God without a pure heart — without paying close attention to this pure heart — principle is naive. Such a one writes times upon quicksand and builds feather castles. For the scriptures are clear; "*Pursue peace with all men, and the sanctification without which no one will see the Lord.*" (Hebrews 12:14). Thus, the eye of the heart must be kept clean of obscurities. The heart must be kept pure if one is to see God and know God as He is.

Beyond Bitterness

This Beatitude is not meant to place God's children under a heavy press and religious burden. Rather, to direct us to keep the channels of our hearts clear of clogging clots so that the oil of God will begin to flow freely. Our hearts must be clear of the muddy water which hinders the flame of God's fire from blazing at its fullest from within. A pure heart does not mean a merely sentimental orientation but a heart bent to repentance, easily touched by God and relating to others in a godly manner. A heart that does not seek to cause damage to others. This is connected to the Beatitude on mourning, as we also read in 2 Corinthians 7:9-11

I now rejoice, not that you were made sorrowful, but that you were made sorrowful to the point of repentance; for you were made sorrowful according to the will of God, so that you might not suffer loss in anything through us. For the sorrow that is according to the will of God produces a repentance without regret, leading to salvation, but the sorrow of the world produces death. For behold what earnestness this very thing, this godly sorrow, has produced in you; what vindication of yourselves, what indignation, what fear, what longing, what zeal, what avenging of wrong! In everything, you demonstrated yourselves to be innocent in the matter.

The purity of heart is a disposition which will not let any wound or bitterness hinder one's clear view of God. It is clarity of thought that holds God in view and spurs the soul beyond all attachment to this passing world. It is a heart that does not hold offense. It is a heart unencumbered by the cares and reputation of this world — not in the sense of rebellion and self-assertion against the move the spirit but a heart which holds on to the possibility of blessing and goodness of God and is gladdened by holy expectation even in the midst of trouble. This pure heart does not stop trusting God to work to raise one high above the circumstances of the world, though it is at the moment in a terrible place. A pure heart is not drawn into bitterness against God or man. It stays focused on the possibility of the outflow of beneficence and the miraculous at every moment. This heart focuses on what is praiseworthy, and consolative.

Holy Spirit and Vigilance

In this world where the battle of heart has become so intense, and the war for the human mind has been turned up to a higher octave, we need God the Holy Spirit to teach us purity of heart. To ask for a pure heart as a gift from the Lord is to ask for the capacity to live in this troubling world and remain a soul unstained by the bitterness it spews. Without a pure heart, there can be no real experience of God in the innermost soul. The purity of heart demands diligence, watchfulness, and alertness.

To have a pure heart we must train ourselves to stand guard at the gateways of our hearts. Set up watch posts on the walls of the city so that our worship flows from a place unsullied by pride, anger, jealousy and all the like.

> *Watch over your heart with all diligence, For from it flow the springs of life. Put away from you a deceitful mouth and put devious speech far from you. Let your eyes look directly ahead and let your gaze be fixed straight in front of you. Watch the path of your feet and all your ways will be established. Do not turn to the right nor to the left; Turn your foot from evil.*
>
> Proverbs 4:23
>
> *My son, give attention to my wisdom, Incline your ear to my understanding;*
>
> Proverbs 5:1

One of the ways to guard our hearts is to obey the voice of the Lord. It is important that we train ourselves to know the voice of the Lord. Exodus 23:21 *"Be on your guard before him and obey his voice; do not be rebellious toward him, for he will not pardon your transgression, since My name is in him."*

Standing Guard

Rebellion sullies the heart and situates one in a place of inner warfare and restlessness toward Him. It may lead to our transgressing legitimate boundaries which have been set up by God. Heart purity is determined by the sound or voice that echoes within it. Jesus said in John 10:27-28 "*My sheep hear My voice, and I know them, and they follow Me; and I give eternal life to them, and they will never perish; and no one will snatch them out of My hand.*"

Scripture implores us to be vigilant over our hearts;

> Psalm 39:1 *I said, "I will guard my ways That I may not sin with my tongue; I will guard my mouth as with a muzzle while the wicked are in my presence."*

> Psalm 141:3 *Set a guard, O Lord, over my mouth; Keep watch over the door of my lips.*

> If we will set the guards of Wisdom, Understanding, Mercy and Justice with the radiance of the Lord to guard our heart, then its eyes will see clearly the King who sits gloriously upon the inner chambers of the heart. "*Do not forsake her, and she will guard you; Love her, and she will watch over you.*" (Proverbs 4:6)

> Ecclesiastes 5:1 *Guard your steps as you go to the house of God, and draw near to listen rather than to offer the sacrifice of fools; for they do not know they are doing evil.*

> Isaiah 21:8 *Then the lookout called, "O Lord, I stand continually by day on the watchtower, And I am stationed every night at my guard post."*

> Isaiah 52:12 *But you will not go out in haste, nor will you go as fugitives; For the LORD will go before you, and the God of Israel will be your rear guard.*

Isaiah 58:8 *Then your light will break out like the dawn, and your recovery will speedily spring forth, and your righteousness will go before you; The glory of the LORD will be your rear guard.*

Micah 7:5 *Do not trust in a neighbor; do not have confidence in a friend. From her who lies in your bosom guard your lips.*

Habakkuk 2:1 *I WILL stand on my guard post and station myself on the rampart, And I will keep watch to see what He will speak to me, And how I may reply when I am reproved.*

Mark 13:9 *But be on your guard; for they will deliver you to the courts, and you will be flogged in the synagogues, and you will stand before governors and kings for My sake, as a testimony to them.*

Luke 12:15 *And He said to them, "Beware, and be on your guard against every form of greed; for not even when one has an abundance does his life consist of his possessions."*

Luke 17:3 *Be on your guard! If your brother sins, rebuke him; and if he repents, forgive him.*

Luke 21:34 *Be on guard, that your hearts may not be weighted down with dissipation and* Acts 20:28 *Be on guard for yourselves and for all the flock, among which the Holy Spirit has made you overseers, to shepherd the church of God which He purchased with His own blood.*

Philippians 4:7 *And the peace of God, which surpasses all comprehension, shall guard your hearts and your minds in Christ Jesus.*

1 Timothy 6:20 *O Timothy, guard what has been entrusted to you, avoiding worldly and empty chatter and the opposing arguments of what is falsely called "knowledge"*

2 Timothy 1:12 *For this reason I also suffer these things, but I am not ashamed; for I know whom I have believed, and I am convinced that He is able to guard what I have entrusted to Him until that day.*

2 Timothy 1:14 *Guard, through the Holy Spirit who dwells in us, the treasure which has been entrusted to you.*

2 Timothy 4:15 *Be on guard against him yourself, for he vigorously opposed our teaching.*

2 Peter 3:17 *You, therefore, beloved, knowing this beforehand, be on your guard lest, being carried away by the error of unprincipled men, you fall from your own steadfastness.*

1 John 5:21 *Little children, guard yourselves from idols.*

Selah.

A Key To Eternity

In this Beatitude, Jesus gave us one of the keys for entering the realm of glory. He gave us a key or frequency that enables us to see beyond the physical and natural - in order to see God. The scripture clearly stated that no one can see God. However, Jesus said that someone can see God but it all depends on the landscape of the heart.

In the Old Testament, the heart and soul are always combined. This explains the fact that your heart is directly connected to your soul. Heart in Hebrew language is spelled as "*lev*" (לֵב).

The heart is a tool. It either brings about growth or destruction. Jesus said the major issue is the heart. The heart is what you carry within you. It's the first place that the Holy Spirit dwells before it goes out to your body. When Jesus was talking about the heart, He referred to it as the gateway to eternity. As we see in Ecclesiastes 3:11;

> *He hath made everything beautiful in his time: also he hath set the world in their heart* (KJV)
>
> *He has made everything appropriate in its time. He has also set eternity in their heart* (NASB)

The Hebrew word for eternity is "*olam*", (עוֹלָם), means *worlds*. It can further be interpreted as you have placed the "*worlds in their hearts*". The access point for the things you are looking for in the world is not on the outside, but inside of your heart. Therefore, if you are searching for something and it does not come to you, you need examine your heart. Most believers make the mistake of thinking that things come to them from the outside. I used to make that mistake too. I used to think that people give me things until the Lord revealed to me that the gateway to receive from anyone is the heart. The structure and position of your heart will determine how people will respond to you. The greatest work you have to do is make sure your heart is clear of clutters. I discovered that if I do not take care of my heart, I run into troubles. This is because people begin to react to me in a certain way based on what is going on inside my heart. I had to start learning how to tune my heart and remove clutters or certain thoughts from my heart so that people can begin to respond to me in a way that is effective for the two parties. This is not an issue of external behavior, rather it's an issue of the heart.

> The soul is God's progeny

A Descendant of Heaven

The heart is so important that God talks about it over 350 times in the Old Testament. It is connected to the soul, and the soul is God's progeny. A believer's soul comes directly from Heaven. The soul you carry now is no longer the one you were born with. The soul you were born with is dead, and you are now reborn from Heaven.

This is why when Jews pray, they pray to thank God for giving them a great soul. People complain that when the Jews pray they thank God for not making them gentiles, but they believe that their souls are hewn from a different place than the gentiles. They believe the gentiles were born from Adam, but they come directly from the throne of God. The Jew, Abraham, and righteousness are the foundations of the world. Since the world is not righteous except through Jesus Christ. For God to be able to bring the Messiah, He had to hewn the souls of the Jews from a different place. Jesus' soul descends from a particular place and this is the place from which you are born again. The place where the souls of the Jews were hewn is where you got born again because that's where the Messiah lives and comes from. Hence, your soul is connected to your heart because your soul must come from eternity into the soul you have. Unbelievers do have souls but their souls are dead. You become a new creature and get reborn from Heaven when you are a believer. Your soul is a direct descendant of the Spirit and sea in Heaven.

The heart is an organ God put in you to pump blood, but it's also a symbol of man's connection to an external realm, the realm of Heaven, and to the things God has put in your heart so it can move to a soul. It is in your heart that the sparks of fire from Heaven ascends and descends. If your heart is clogged, the fire becomes lukewarm. If the heart is wicked, the fire goes out and the gate closes. You can either receive from Heaven flowing from the superior realm, or from Hell flowing from the inferior realm.

The heart opens up to eternity but it does not just open up to the eternal realm where God is, rather it also opens up to the realm where evil dwells. Hence, the Bible can talk about the possibility of having a pure heart and, at the same time, say the heart is desperately wicked. It talks about all the wickedness that comes out from the heart of man. The heart is a tool that God made to have access to eternity, now because you have been reborn from above. Hence, you have to deepen your awareness of how your heart functions. You need to look deep into it and find out what happens, how its structures work, how it brings forth speech, and how its imagination works — because God said the heart thinks, talks, and imagines.

The Originator of Thought and Cosmic Travel

Therefore, there is no speech in your tongue, no image in your imagination or thought in your heart unless it has been in your heart. Your heart sends electric impulses more than the brain. The heart, in sending electric impulses, is the originator of thoughts. The thoughts come from the realm outside of a human being, so if the heart is messed up the person can't think right. Sin does not dwell in the head but in the heart.

Physically, the heart is connected to everything, as it's connected to your body, hence your body is also associated as to how your heart is connected to the cosmos. Remember, your heart has a gate into eternity. He has placed worlds in your heart, so it has a connection to the worlds. Every cosmic pattern, galaxy and planetary system in the world can feel your heartbeat because, if your heart did not have worlds, your soul can't travel. You need to consider and become aware of how your heart connects to God, how it affects the cosmos, how it shapes your daily life and the lives of others, how it can open and close dimensions for you, and how it can either affect an environment to your detriment or health.

If the heart can have all these qualities and can still be desperately wicked, people should not be told to follow their hearts. It's dangerous telling anyone to do that because most people do not know the voice of their heart distinctly from God. You could tell someone to follow their heart, but it will be filled with carnality and unrighteousness. You should follow the Spirit and eternity, and not your heart. The reason why so many people fail in what they do is because they follow their hearts. You have to know what someone's heart is like first before you can tell him to follow his heart. Believers can be told to follow their hearts because Christ lives in their hearts. However, most do not listen to the Christ in their heart, rather they listen to themselves.

The heart's integrated connection to the cosmos is a powerful thing. Scientists are realizing that the magnetic field of the heart is larger than that of the brain. Your heart senses things. When people have problems they do not have a brain attack, but a heart attack. They may get sick in the brain as a result of certain things, but the heart reacts instantly to things that are in its environment. This is because its sensory organs are heightened. When someone becomes a believer, their heart becomes specifically heightened. They become so sensitive because their hearts have been sensitized. The gates of eternity are opened for them. However, you have to learn the act of discipleship. The act of discipleship entails training yourself to be sensitive to God but not too sensitive to humans.

You need to really enter the spirit realm to understand the mysterious working of the human heart. There are certain things people will do that are not right. They are smart, so it becomes surprising they end up doing the wrong things. This should simply tell you that people do not know what is not good for them! The Jews say it is the demon that sits on the left side of your chest, standing at the side of the ventricle of your heart. It takes ascendancy and pulls you to the inferior realm. You will start to react from that realm and not from your upper nature. It always seems to work against your best interest.

> Make your heart free from clutter

Creating Out of No Thing

The first thing I discovered as I started reading the passage "blessed are the pure in heart" is that all the frequencies of the passage have the "seven word form". The seven-word form is a principle of creation and awakening.

713 and 714 are numbers for creation and awakening because creation is that which brings something out of no thing and turns it into something. It is that which quickens or awakens that which is asleep or dead. Real creation brings something out of no thing, hence, your heart is a space by which the things that do not

exist can come into existence. It is a vessel for drawing from the supernatural realm to the physical realm.

God said David is a man after his own heart. In Hebrew, his name is spelt "dalet vav dalet" (דָּוִד Dawid) but in some places it's spelt as "dalet vav yod dalet". "Dalet vav" means to *worship* or *bend towards* something. "Da", in my first language, means to fall or move towards something. While, 'Yid' is to give something out of love to someone. God was saying David's heart is bent towards Him. The heart is the principle by which we are bent towards Him. The church teaches Jesus is in your heart. Jesus told us that He is the way, truth, and life. Therefore, Jesus is in my heart simply means that there is a door within a door that allows things from the other realm to come to you.

Your heart is different from the heart of the world. The biggest task is making your heart free from clutters, not going to bed with grudges or the wrong thoughts, and not listening to what people say. Your heart is important. The heart can be a hindrance and can prevent what you need from coming to you. However, it does not mean you are condemned; there's always a cure or healing.

Be Free

You can tell how much somebody has grown in a relationship when something is refused. For a young married couple, the test of a relationship is always when the person says "no". Then you have to determine whether you are in this for love or for what you get from the relationship. You have to be free enough for your wife to say "not tonight" and you still have joy and love. If you do not learn this, God is going to keep repeating it in your life. He's going to make you a millionaire one day and take it away the next month, just to teach you how to relate to Him. Not that God does not love you, but it is because something is in you that needs to be free. God will not sacrifice your freedom for things. If He cannot train you on how to be free, He cannot make you a prophet.

The Church in American has lost its prophetic impulse because it does not want the government to take away its finance. The church has been sorcerized. The church has been bamboozled. We have to understand that if we do not come to the place of freedom, we cannot speak as prophets. We can only be sycophants - somebody who thinks that proximity to power equals power and that by singing the praise of someone who is in power it gives them power. This what the whole church is doing. The point is we have to be free! How can we be prophetic if we are not free? It is a matter of the heart. Because the heart determines what happens in nature and in society.

Olam

The heart is the alchemical center where God puts His ingredient for transformation. So the heart is the organ in the physical body that pulls everything together and feeds everything. All that has been created and that which shall be created is accessible to the heart. It does not say "world", but it says "worlds", — which is eternity. So if eternity is accessible to the heart, it means that even the things that are not yet created by God are accessible to the heart.

In Sunday School you were taught that God lives in your heart. This is just a simple way of letting you know that your heart is the Tabernacle of infinity. And then Jesus tells you that the Kingdom of God that is within you. What He is actually referring to is your heart. You walk around the world carrying the world in your heart. It is not the world that carries you, but you carry the world. Therefore, it is not the world that forms you, but you form the world!

Governing The Worlds

God says guard your heart because out of it are the issues of life (Proverbs 4:23). It does not say that "out of it are the issues of your life", but "out of it are the issues of life". Your heart is the place where everything that happens in life that is perceptible, that you can see, originates. So if there is wickedness in the society, it came from your heart. It is not that which goes into a man's heart that actually corrupts him. It is that which comes out — for out of the heart comes wickedness, comes robbery, comes fornication, comes killing, comes murder (Matthew 15:19). So in other words, the things that are in the society are not the fault of Hollywood, but is the fault of your heart!

The issue is that the heart of man has become so corrupt, even believers have been infected by corruption. If a believer's heart were actually pure the way it is supposed to be, the world would be pure. The world will be framed in a way of purity.

Do not tell me that the reason we have all this pornography is because there are a few people in Hollywood who think that way. No, it is because a majority of people, including people in the church, think that way. I am sorry. I am not saying this to condemn anyone, but I want to let you know how powerful it is when God actually comes to live in your heart and what He is trying to do. If a tyrannical ruler rises in a nation, it is because the heart of the people have tuned it that way.

It has nothing to do with the color. It has to do with the heart. It has nothing to do with the nation, it has nothing to do with America, Nigeria or Russia. It has to do with the heart — because out of the heart are the issues of life! And so God comes to tell Israel: "You shall love the Lord your God with all your heart" (Deuteronomy 6:5; Matthew 22:37; Mark 12:30; Luke 10:27). God did not put spirit first. There is no spirit in that law. It did not say "You shall love The Lord your God with your spirit". It is not there. It is "with all your heart, and with all your soul, and with all your strength", and Jesus comes and says "mind." There is no spirit there. The first reference is to the heart! The reason God wants to sit in your heart is that, by sitting there, He becomes the filter of the things that come from eternity into time.

The problem is we push God away from the heart, and we enthrone something else. We remove God from the center of our heart and things flow through that are not filtered by the love of God.

The heart from the perspective of Scripture is that instrument which is not just a natural organ. The heart represents that instrument that vibrates and resonates to tune creation to what a human being needs (or perceives that he needs). Your heart will tune the world according to your desire. So if your job in your house is to fight with everybody and to quarrel every day, then you are making your heart tune the world for your own quarreling. It becomes a hindrance to what you think is good for you. You believed you were thinking in your head and not in your heart, but that's not true. *"For as he thinketh in his heart, so is he"* (Proverbs 23:7 KJV).

This has to do with the framing of the world. This has to do with the framing of the universe. It has nothing to do with you being able to think, structure and tinker with artificial matters. That's for your head to do. The organizing of data comes from your head. The forming of the world comes from your heart, because it is the heart that frames the universe. (It does not mean you do not use your logic).

Know Your Heart

Why is it that we think things should be different but they remain the same? Why is it that what we think it is, is not what it is? Because there are two sets of thought. One frames the world and the other collects and analyzes data. So if a heart is filled with hatred, no matter how much we think the world should be different, the world will be based on what is in our heart. So if there is racism in a country, it is because that is what is in the heart. We can lie all we want to lie. We can pretend it is not there but it is there because that is what is in our heart. If there's rape in a country, it is because it is in the heart of people. If there is misogyny, it is in the heart of people. I am not trying to make you uncomfortable. We have to return to the heart of the matter — the heart! It is not something else. It is not somebody else. It is you. It is me. It is us!

When I examine my heart, I see things in it, I wonder how it gets there. So I start learning how not to lie to myself. So the first thing we should have learned in Sunday School is "Thou shall not lie to yourself." What makes us impure are the lies we tell ourselves in the depth of our being. One truth told to the heart can heal the world, but we haven't got there because we do not tell ourselves the truth. We live in the world of make-believe and looking-good. We refuse to look at ourselves, to look at the heart.

"The heart is more deceitful than all else and is desperately sick; Who can understand it?" (Jeremiah 17:9) Since I understood what was said through Jeremiah, I have come to the point of constantly telling my heart "Do not lie to me!" I have to acknowledge with God that if I am not careful, the complexity of the heart will get me in a corner and convince me that I am who I am not. Who makes me think my sin is not the same as everybody else's sin? So I do not confess because I do not commit sin. "My sin?..... Oh, that was not a sin, it was a mistake!" An open confession is more healing than you pretending that you do not have an issue.

> Tell yourself the truth

I used to quarrel with my wife until one day the Lord said to me, "Son, can you look into your heart?" He knows me because Jesus lives in my heart. The Lord continued, "I choose to live in a dirty place. It does not mean your heart is clean, it just means that I choose to live in it." It hit me really hard! My whole idea was since the Lord lives in me, it must be clean! He said, "Son, no!" "God demonstrates His own love toward us, in that while we were yet sinners..."(Romans 5:8). He came to even me with all the junk in me! I kept saying, "God, I thought when you came, my sins are over." God said, "Look, I used the Blood of my Son to cover it and to cleanse it, but it's still there. You have not dealt with it." I said, "Jesus took it away!" He confronted me "Why did you do this and that?" I was shocked. He then said, "It is because you do not tell your heart the truth ... And ye shall know the truth, and the truth shall make you free. See, you are not allowing the truth to make you free. I will keep living in your heart. I will keep loving you. But you are going to keep being in bondage because you do not tell yourself the truth."

You got to tell yourself the truth. Telling yourself the truth is looking at the issue in its face and saying "I know who you are. You want to be a star in front of everybody else, and you refuse to have a relationship with the Lord and you refuse to have a Truth relationship with yourself." I am telling you this so you will understand God lives in your heart. You want to tell the Truth so your heart is able to manifest the things you actually are thinking about in the world. The only time it will let go of an error is when the truth is told to it.

The cognitive power of the heart is so deep that it directs the nerves of the universe. Its intelligence is so vast, it records everything. The heart, because of the lies we tell it, and because of our refusal to look at its deceitful nature, creates fragmentations within and without. When the heart receives Truth, it becomes integral, that is it brings everything together.

It is interesting that God says, "purify your hearts, you double-minded." (James 4:8). In other words, let your heart in Truth speak, and you speak only one thing - the Will of God. It is in speaking that 'one thing' that your heart is pure.

Your heart is talking from places that you are not in control of. Even if you try to control it, it will still be beyond your control, because it is familiar spirits. The only thing that deals with familiar spirits is the Truth. You do not need to cast them out. Because if you keep casting them out, they keep coming back. They won't go anywhere. They are in the heart. That's why they are called familiar spirits because it is the result of familiar relationships.

God is Love

How do you purify your heart? By keeping the commandments. But there is only one commandment — to love.

"the love of God has been poured out within our hearts through the Holy Spirit who was given to us." (Romans 5:5). In other words, the heart receives love as a balm or as a terraforming instrument. "So if I can get my heart to truly love..." Is it that simple? I know you think you know how to love? That's what I thought, too. Then I realized I need to become Love, not even learn how to love. Because the Bible says God is Love. It is a very simple lesson.

Let's get back to the basics: God is love! Love is the essential nature of God. It is who God is, not what God does. So, if love is what God is, that means when God enters an environment, the environment changes by the presence of love. If you walk into an environment and it does not change, you do not have love. You are not love! There are times when I am loved and there are times when I am not loved because of the things that I think I am not. I can tell the difference. When you become love, you do not have to work so hard because if you are loved, you do not have to struggle to be kind. If you are loved, you do not have to struggle to be pure. As we know, if you are love, you are God!

1 Corinthians 13 speaks of going to heaven and gallivanting with seraphim, and yet you are not God because your love is sporadic. You love one time and then you are your old self the next time. You are saying you want to be God but God gives you the simplest way of being Him and you can't even do it. God didn't ask you to kill yourself to be like Him. He did not ask you to create angels to be like Him. He didn't ask you to go to hell, beat the Devil, pull him up and punch his daylights out to be like Him. He didn't ask you to create worlds so that you would be like Him. Instead, to be like your Father in Heaven, be love!

The Mystic Way

Selfishness is not love. If you really love yourself, you won't be selfish. Love nullifies you. That is, when you have love, you do not exist anymore. You become God. That is the mystic way. Love is the only thing that unites people and causes one to disappear into the other person.

When you actually become love, boundaries get dissolved. It is not because you are meandering into people's mess, but rather your presence dissolves boundaries. Because walls do not hold God back, rivers do not stop God from crossing, fires do not burn God, hatred does not move God. I want to be like my Father. I want to be God. Not in the sense of ruling the world and telling everybody what to do. No, I want to be truly God. Even to the people who are putting their finger into God's eye. When they put their finger into God's eye, the juice runs through their body and provides nourishment.

Love is the transmutative power that changes the world. Love is the garment of eternity in time. Love is the movement of God into the fullness of existence. Love is what allows you to have a mystic gaze into what cannot be seen. Love is the illuminative principle. Love is the transformational gaze. When you look at people with love, they change without your saying anything. Love is the light waves upon which the angels fly. Love is the intensity of the spirit exalting those who are downtrodden.

Jesus said "But if thine eye be evil, thy whole body shall be full of darkness" (Matthew 6:23 KJV). If your eyes be pure, all things become pure. That means the way you see purifies what you look at. Love is the way of seeing. If you are in love, you look at the person differently and you have no idea how that perception changes that person, and changes you too!

Love is immortality

> Protect your heart

"The Love of God is shed abroad in your heart" (Romans 5:5 KJV) to cause worlds to come, to frame worlds, to purify worlds. Because only love can do that. For the heart to be able to do so, you need to tell the heart the Truth. You cannot allow things that are not God to sit on your heart for too long. The only way you can become God is through love. There is no other way because love is also light. And light is life.

If I had not been through it, I could not talk to you about it. Revelation is one thing but experience is another. I have decided to love in a way that I have not done before. When I am in the presence of people, they know when I cut them into pieces trying to remove the junk that is inside, they still know that I love them. Before this revelation, what I did was go into a place and pronounced "in three days... judgment." I have done it to cities. I have done it to people. "I give you nine months. If you do not change, the Lord will take you home." I did not know how to intercede. I just gave the message. I have learned a lot in the past 45 years. I know that love conquers all. "Many waters cannot quench love ... Love is stronger than death," (Song of Solomon 8). That's why I say love is immortality.

De-Cluttering

The Evangelicals and the Pentecostals have a problem with emptying the mind, because they think they are being demonic. So they carry all the clutter of the mind to Heaven. Without emptying the mind, it is filled with all kinds of junk and you get familiar spirits. I am not saying "demonic," but "familiar spirits," — the written codes of your family's conversations inside your heart. And you carry all this up there and you want to tailor Heaven accordingly. Then you wonder how come nothing is coming with me when I come down? Well, you went into an unlimited space with a limited vessel. The vessel of the mind is so limited that it cannot even contain your own thought. So if you want to actually bring down from that Heavenly realm to this realm, the space inside of you must correspond to the space inside of God.

It is amazing how we train ourselves to become our own hindrances, and we have called it religion. We actually call it spirituality! When you want to go to Heaven, stop the carrying of pre-conceived images up. All images are fleeting, especially when most of us cannot hold an image for two seconds. I mean the actual ideas that flow from the realm of nothingness we cannot hold, which is why Christians have a hard time being inventors. In order to hold a new Heavenly image, you need to have a capacity of self-emptying. It is a hard task! Remember, the biggest task is to clarify what you desire.

The next biggest task is to release your being from all the things that you are cluttered with, so that you can become a space where God can form His own imagery — not what you make Him to become. All this is in the heart. You can begin by centering the heart. I like the old monastic-centering prayers. It is about the structures of the heart and opening the gates of the heart. Your heart is so important, both to you and to God.

This your heart is in the שׁ (Shin), with four chambers. Your heart is the Sabbath of God, because this is where God comes to rest. That's the whole idea — for God to rest there! The heart is the recipient of the Rivers of Eden. The river went from Eden and watered the Garden and broke into four. Your heart receives those four rivers. Your heart carries for you access to everything you will ever need. It can be fomented in the laboratory of your heart. Anything! It is where we can foment or fashion things for manifestations.

In the realm where God is, there are no images. Images are a result of God interacting with you and the images return back to nothingness after every time they reveal. You cannot permanize images in the realm of the being with God Himself. Your heart is the place where God brings the images. When you enter into God, release everything and return to yourself, your heart takes what has been seen in the unseen, the "what is not", and foments it into something that is usable, the 'what is'. If the heart operates the way it is supposed to operate, it serves as a holographic projection of what was not into what is. Your heart can then become a hindrance, because the seed can die in the gateway of the heart. Or it can be buried there and can never be pulled out. Jesus said, "*Blessed are the pure in heart.*" It is not about lust. It is not about thinking bad thoughts, in the sense of how we think. Purity is about making the heart a place for forming images that are not detrimental to your own wellbeing.

Creating From Gold

Protect your heart, but not from loving people. For those of you who have had your hearts broken, you may protect your hearts to not let anybody to ever come in anymore. That will be part of the issue you are having right now, because you have just created a laboratory for the incapacity to receive. Purity of heart is the opening of the heart to the dimensions of the worlds, the opening of the heart to all possible worlds. The allowing of the heart to be the gateway for the worlds that are still getting ready to be born to come into this realm.

Considering the four Rivers of Eden, Pison, the one that had gold, is the river of overflowing abundance that carries the particle of abundance that can become whatever one needs because that is what gold does. Gold informs the realm! The Bible says the gold of that land is good. The word for gold zahab (זָהָב) is not really hard gold, but soft gold, which means it is "gold at an empty state". It is gold that can vibrate at a certain level that can do all kinds of things. It was living. It was alive! It could actually give life.

The gold that surrounded the Ark of the Covenant was alive. Do you remember? The Ark bearers took the Ark somewhere and the Ark just decided, "I want to mess up this place!" It was alive! It was treated like a being. It was carried about as a king!

Your heart carries the same thing according to God, at least in the metaphorical sense. It carries that life! Here is a secret. This gold we talk about could cause anything to grow. It was so powerful it could renew the body. The legend of it was so strong the Europeans were looking for it in India. (Because, really, the First River is the Ganges! I will leave that alone. Look at all the legends in Europe, they thought the people in India never died. There are all these legends of the people in that area, how they did this, how they did that, which are true! Do you think there is not the memory in the head of humanity about what this gold really is? They were going to the East to look for it!). When the Magi came, they brought living gold. What they brought to Jesus was a living thing, because you never hear about it again.

Jesus says, "*out of the abundance of the heart the mouth speaketh*" (Matthew 12:34 KJV). So what do you want to do in the world? You carry it with you — not in the hands of the president, not in the hand of the government — it is in the heart of man. Some of the church in America, the Evangelical and the Pentecostals, have a heart that is uncaring. The heart does more damage than the hands do. So we must now turn to the alchemy of the heart and begin to reformulate how we want the world to be formed.

Pouring Out On The Earth

Part of the ascension activities we do is to make sure your heart, by looking from the perspective above, becomes a crucible, a container for decanting and creating good liquor on earth. That is what the Gospel does! It is the casting of a word of goodness, and it is directed by the chambers of the heart. Oh God, help my heart! Something I have learnt a long time ago, and keep learning it over and over again, is that every time my heart vibrates a certain frequency, I get the result of what I carry in my heart, whether I like it or not. So I am learning how to guard my heart and what I say.

In the 70's and the 60's, there were tests in Harvard on heroin and LSD and their effects. Can a human being, by using drugs, reprogram themselves, their bodies and reprogram everything. They made a lot of mistakes, but one of the things that I learnt by reading all their work, is that by moving in the spirit, I can program my heart to actually give off waves that impacts people positively. So I guard my mouth, because the gate of the mouth is connected with the gate of the heart. You can do so much. God lives in your heart and your heart carries that gold from the land that is good and can grow anything.

We talk about the Nile, the Blue Nile, which is what is mentioned as Gihon. There are two sources of the Nile, one in Uganda, the other one in Ethiopia. One is called the White Nile, the other one is called the Blue Nile. The one that is talked about here is the Blue Nile. As the Asians call it, the Sapphire Nile, which was used to have a reference to the Sea of Glass. Ethiopia is a Christian nation. It is the only nation of earth that has not been conquered from outside. The only nation that has not been conquered from outside is a Christian nation. It has been Christian since the 1st century. It is a nation on Earth that is a sign of what is possible. Look at the church that is inside the Nile, that actually is used for creating sounds and the ancients used it to tune the Earth. I will leave it right here.

> The world needs you

"I love your heart. I just love you," I have said to myself, "I am not having conversation about anybody that does not have anything to do with love." I do not care how right I think I am. I want to have a conversation of about what I want to see happen, not what is happening. I want to tune my heart as the lab, the alchemical port, to become a place where the good drink is made and the people who drink from it to be drunk and have joy. Remember, what you carry in that heart you carry around, the world needs you. Leave your politics behind you. The world needs you.

It is not necessarily a good thing that we have born-again Christians in a cabinet. Stop thinking that this is the Kingdom of God, it is not. Stop thinking just because there are Christians in power, it makes everything okay. It does not work like that. You are the one who changes creation. Remember power corrupts, and absolute power corrupts absolutely. The reason you can change with purity is because you do not have the political power — you have the spiritual power! You can operate from the place of detached love. You can! You are the one who is able to see the heart of God — for the stranger and for the citizen, for the orphan and for the child in the family, for the widow and or for the married woman, for the poor and for the rich. You have the capacity to see that. You are not beclouded by power.

Do not get yourself beclouded by the idea of proximity to power. You are different. Your heart carries a different vibration. That is what you should be releasing. Release it over the nation. I am praying for the Church. I am praying for God's people, Note that a law passed by people who claim to know God can do more harm (because of who they are) than a law passed by a nonbeliever. The non-believer has a limitation that the believer does not have. I am more scared of believers in power than I am scared of unbelievers. A believer who goes astray can do greater damage than anybody in the world. An immature believer can destroy the world. An immature unbeliever can only destroy himself.

A Benediction

Just know who you are. Do not forget who you are. God loves you. You have such a great heart, an incredible heart. Forgive yourself! Forgive your heart! Release all the accusations said to you, "You are not a person. You are a messenger from the new age. Glory cannot land on you. It will not attach itself to you".

They said you will never be able to do it. They said it is not going to work because you are a woman. They said it is not going to work because the money is not going to come for the project. Release that, because by releasing it, it is coming. Your heart is in denial. You said it is in the future. That's not true. Something was spoken. And the chambers of your heart carry it. The gold of that land is good.

Forgive everyone. Release your heart. Your heart is too important. There is a new world that wants to come through your heart. Release everyone. Release the disappointment. Release it. It's okay. Let it go. Release it. You feel that wave. Release it. You that you have been laboring to have certain things manifest, issues you have been moving around in the spirit realm to bring forth, and this is going to be a new season for you. Your whole body system begins to open up dimensions that draws into this realm what has been in your heart all these years. You will see it even more. Just release the anxiety from your heart. Release it. Forgive them. Do not let anybody stand in the gateway of your heart, it is okay to stand for what was placed in you for eternity, to begin to be realized here.

There is something said about you before Creation, "You carry the fullness of Who I AM."

7TH BEATITUDE

7th Beatitude, Blessed are the peacemakers

Blessed are the Peacemakers, for they shall be called the sons of God

Matthew 5:9

The blessedness of peacemaking is understood in the harmonic divine frequency which holds the cosmos in integral interconnection.

Peacemaking also is the capacity to remove destructive elements, pathologies, and the negative twisting with divine skill without disintegrating the whole or disentangling from divinely necessary entanglements through which people, systems, and worlds sustain life and love. It is to bring harmonic interaction without bringing about the separation in which interconnections are lost and genuine relationships die forever. The peacemaker is the one who finds the still center in themselves that carries the divine harmonic resonance from which they draw and release peace upon the world and people.

Peacemaking is not the result of knowing exactly how conflict came to be, but having an intuitive sense of the need for equilibrium, knowing instinctively that disequilibrium is present though often not spoken. Peace is not searching for the guilt of culprits of the disequilibrium, though many will want the peacemaker to assign blame. However, assigning blame does not release lasting peace; rather, it postpones the inevitable conflict. Peacemaking is a spiritual shift of force to tilt the universe back to harmonic equilibration by the peace of God which passes understanding dwelling within the man or woman of peace.

I must emphasize that peacemaking is first of all *your* peace, which is *your* responsibility. Peace is primarily a gift which is given and that must be received and preserved by an inner working of the one who intends to make peace. The Beatitude is almost circuitous. Far be it from me to accuse the Lord and Master of making a circuitous argument, but I think it is intended to be circuitous. Read it again: "Blessed are the peacemakers for they shall be called the sons of God." Some versions have "children." I think that the word "children" understates the weight of the responsibility of peacemaking and detracts from the cosmic responsibilities of the those who are born of God. The circuitous nature of the argument is that if you are not already a son, you cannot be a peacemaker. Peacemaking is written in the core hardware of what it means to be a son of God, that is, if we take our cue from the begotten Son of God, Jesus Christ, our

Lord and Master states it another way, "My peace I give to you." This peace is given based on sonship and relational entangling with God through the blood of the Son. That one's peace is one's own responsibility is clear. It is a choice that one must make to be at peace with God and hence within one's self. Until this peace is experienced within, any external move to make peace is just a seed sown for future conflicts and restlessness. Only when we have peace can we make peace.

Since peace is necessary for being a son of God, it behooves us then to be more attuned to peace. One who has not possessed or been grasped by the peace Christ gives cannot get very far with peacemaking, be it interpersonal or international. True inner peace is not merely a sense of calm, but the actual distillation of God's inner rest into one's life. It is the ground for peace-living and peacemaking. This means that there is a certain spiritual awareness that forms the foundation of lived peace which then leads to peacemaking. This lived peace and being at or in peace within oneself alters our inner nature, moving us from agitation to the restful embrace of life, from anxiety to the trustful embrace of divine providence, from bitterness to the sweetness of divine love and forgiveness, from projective self-defense to lived divine harmonic resonance. In this resonance, peace is not merely the cessation of external conflict but the harmonization of the inner worlds with all its ebb and flow dancing to divine frequencies in divine synchronicity. It is through the process of peace that the self emerges in its newness and continually recreates of all things. It is peace that sustains the foundation of being. For a human being, the necessity of having a sustained peace between body, soul, and the Divine spirit cannot only be the function of an unconscious need to survive, but it must also be intentional and focused, drawing from the depth of God. Because the world is in constant flux and restlessness, it is in constant conflict with itself. It cannot be at peace unless the man of peace, who is a son of God, shows up. Its current structures and movements cannot be the basis of peacemaking. The decision

> This lived peace and being at or in peace within oneself alters our inner nature

to surrender one's being into the Holy One when truly affected by His peace causes one to sit in the place that allows one to be a "Peacemaker."

The gate of peace which leads to sonship is the supernal pathway taken by the weary and battered, and they are immediately in the presence of the Holy One. Peace is grounded in love and humility which form the basis of non-agitation. The personal hell which many experience within is often the result of vexation and inner agitation caused by anger and anxious living. Anger, of course, is known for its capacity to remove peace and block the way of divine serenity. Anxious living is most often caused by fear that robs one of their inner peace and, consequently, this person is grounded in human rebellion against God. It follows then that the first way to open the way of peace is through atonement and repentance. YHVH spends a great time in the Torah speaking to Israel about making peace offerings and sacrifices of atonement.

When one makes peace, especially with God, it gives rise to health and healing. In turn, peace with God and healing the relationship between God and man gives rise to the revelation of abundance.

Just as agitation and anxiety arising out of guilt blocks the way of life and often releases destruction and loss, so returning to peace and peacemaking causes restoration to spring forth. A true peacemaker then is the cosmic restorer of the lost fortunes of creation and humanity. When one is truly a peacemaker and peacemaking is not merely external gamesmanship, breaches in them and in the world around them are rebuilt to restore the inflow of the original internal peace which existed before only in the triune God. The peacemaker is not merely a restorer of lost fortunes but the creator of new ones for by them and through the gateway of peace in their heart, he/she calls forth from eternal realms new modes of being that repair the world and prepare creation to move towards that which has never been. As it is written. "Eye has not seen, ear has not heard, neither has it entered into the heart of man what God has prepared for those who love him and are called according to His purpose." (1 Corinthians 2:9)

Those who love him are those who have peace with Him and embody His peace. They are the pathways for manifesting that which eye has not seen or ear heard. These peacemakers are also the ones who are called according His purpose which is to plant everlasting peace upon creation, a peace whose foundation He laid by the blood of his Son Jesus Christ. In this way, they rebuild the primordial foundation of harmonic divine resonance which they carry within and transfer to creation and humanity.

God is the ultimate peacemaker. We know He is constantly seeking to make peace with humanity. And He knows that the only peace that can become real in the center of the human being is to cleanse them from all their iniquity which has closed the paths of peace within. "They have sinned against Me, and I will pardon all their iniquities by which they have sinned against Me and by which they have transgressed against Me" He says through the mouth of Jeremiah.

Where a true peacemaker is present there is a raising of joy, praise, and glory. Every peacemaker is a healer of nations of the earth. They are prone to elicit good news. When the sound of their frequency is heard, there stirs within the hearts of men, women, and children an intimation of the good omen from the God of heaven. There is no easier way to remove fear and terror than to make peace. A true peacemaker carries within and around them the Spirit of the Fear of the LORD who calls forth fear and trembling in the heart of the wicked and the unjust who have taken advantage of the weak. Thus, we come to the fact that peacemaking is not for cowards but for the bold of heart—those who have been made righteous and whose boldness is like lion. Peacemakers strike terror into the heart of the wicked because they know that the river of glorious goodness that arises from peace is about to flow and its wake of oppression is carried away. In this world, most people, including religious and spiritual people, don't want peacemaking. And as sad as it makes me to say it, especially religious people frequently eschew peacemaking and thus delay the eternal and original purpose of God.

The peacemaker is the one who by *being* and *doing* causes

"*Olam haba* to become *Olam hazeh.*" They cause, by their mode of being, the world to become this present world. They are the embodiment of "thy Kingdom come." It is no longer just said "the days are coming," but that *these* are the days of the Lord's fulfillment of His good will which He spoke when he created man in His image and His likeness, peace between the man and the woman, peace between the man and the beast, peace between the suns and the moons, peace between the stars of light and the mysteries of darkness, peace between Israel and the nations. As I have said, if the peacemakers arise and the gates of eternal peace are opened, it shall no longer be said in *those* days, but *those* days shall become *these* days. In fact it is these days for those who believe that in this age and time God has caused "the righteous Branch of David to spring forth." His coming has ushered in the execution of justice and righteousness on the earth but only peacemakers can harvest its fruits. For Jerusalem to become Jeru-*Shalom* and to dwell in safety, there must arise those who are peacemakers whose being is structured according to peace, whose secret name is YHVH-*Shalom* which is the name YHVH-*Tzidkenu*. The mystery of this name is the righteousness of righteousness. It is the hidden mystery of the Lord in the seed of David who shall be the man who sits on the throne of the house of Israel. The peaceful shall eat the fruit of the tree that grows from the tree of that throne and drink of the springs of life that spring forth from the root of the throne, as the mystery says.

> call for the peace that is everlasting

By the mouth of His prophets he makes clear that this peacemaking is not a temporary soothing of angst nor a temporal cessation of conflict. By Ezekiel He says,

> [26] "I will make a covenant of peace with them; it will be an everlasting covenant with them. And I will place them and multiply them and will set My sanctuary in their midst forever.
>
> [27] "My dwelling place also will be with them; and I will be their God, and they will be My people.

> [28] "And the nations will know that I am the LORD who sanctifies Israel, when My sanctuary is in their midst forever."'"
>
> Eze 37:26-28 NAU

The blessedness of the peacemaker is that, as sons, they call for the peace that is everlasting. It is not merely a quest for a temporal lull in conflict but the weaving of a cosmic thread of the simple process of daily peacemaking into the eternal realm. Peacemakers understand that every movement toward peace that is derived from the righteousness and justice of the Holy One, even when it is just between two brethren, casts its net eternally. If we grasp that Israel is the cosmic seed and the cosmic matrix by which the Holy One enters and sustains the world, a covenant of peace with Israel and her beleaguered scattered people reverberates throughout the cosmos when done based on the righteousness of and justice of the holy and not from mere sentimentality. Why does the passage above say, "They shall be my people and I shall be their God"? Were they not already his people? It will then seem that both internal and external peace are marks of an authentic relationship and define the depth of the relationship of God and people.

As has been stated before, the blessedness of the peacemaker is not just attributed to them by virtue of being called sons of God, but in the effect of their peacemaking ontology on others in the world. This ontic peace has this amazing power to transmute tribulation through joy into glory. It is not typical for us to think of peace as an instrument to attain victory. We often think of peace mainly as an after-effect of certain activities, but peace ontologized in the inner realm is a weapon of victory. That restful calm that comes from within allowing those who embody the peace required to overcome the world was spoken of by the Lord Jesus Christ when he said,

> [33] "These things I have spoken to you, so that in Me you may have peace. In the world you will have tribulation, but take courage; I have overcome the world."
>
> John 16:33 NAU

It seems to me that the Lord Jesus Christ is giving this peace as a way for the believer to live victoriously over the troubles of this world. It is the instrument of their victory and the transmitter of the joy of an overcoming life. The peacemaker is really one who has the capacity to transfer their peace to others around them and create a serenity that empowers them in their daily lives. Peace is then a precursor to cosmic joy. Peace is transcendental because it is something that the world cannot give. Christ says in John 14:27,

> "Peace I leave with you; My peace I give to you; not as the world gives do I give to you. Do not let your heart be troubled, nor let it be fearful."

Peace is an activator and conveyor of the presence of the risen Lord, if we cultivate peace we cultivate the presence. Practicing peace is practicing the presence. Practice provides a protective covering of the *Ruach Hakodesh* upon those who carry this peace. Someone who is practiced in peace can transcend their geographical limitation and touch another person miles away and in many cases change and transform their condition by that presence. The Master here lets us know that peace is transferable from one person to another. Because He carried this peace, and He is the Prince of Peace, He can promise His presence to His disciples. Often we want to be present with those whom we love spiritually, but we tend to do so with profound lack of peace, and so we are unable to reach them, try as we may. However, the Master who knows the secret shows here that by giving peace and having peace we can remain connected at distances too great to fathom. We are often unable to touch each other not because we lack care, but often because we have no peace and are therefore incapable of giving peace.

As for peace as a protective covering, in the portion which has been cited above we see that He moves from this idea of the giving of peace to telling them

> "... for the ruler of the world is coming, and he has nothing in Me;"
>
> John 14:30 NAU

Peace is perfection and essential to the deification process. Those who are at peace are not subject to fate and fatalism. Peacemaking is then the deliverance of humanity from fatalism—particularly that fate which binds the human soul to perpetual inner and external conflicts. For the true cessation of strife is disentangling from slavery to agitation and death that is so common to humanity in this present state. Such peace is not humanity's by their current natural tendency, nor is it present in creation. As a matter of fact, harmonic peace is purchased temporally by the destruction of that which stands in its way even when, by all appearances, that which stands in the ways is good and could eventually engender peace. But humanity assumes that what is, is the way things ought to be, especially in the area of social-political interaction. Rather, peace is gifted by God and heaven and it can only be made if it is so gifted. It is in peace that man's true freedom is exercised. Hence, the man or woman who is perfectly free is at peace within the self and with God.

Peace when attained through its given-ness produces reverence and beauty. When one is blinded by conflict, internally or externally, everything around seems ugly and terrifying. And those who make the spiritual journey mainly a matter of conflict lose a sense of the peace and harmony that is meant to transform and transmute the world. Creation from destruction and conflict is not the ideal divine process, which is why all evil comes from agitation, never from true peace. Sin is often the result of restlessness. Since everything creates according to its nature, what is created from peace and by peace leads to peace. Whatever is created from destruction always carries within it the seed of destruction no matter how it is refined. That means that peace must be the very nature of the one who makes peace. They are drawn into the inner being of God and find within that center of rest and stillness where knowing of God is immediate and intuitive. From this place, they are the ones who can make such peace.

In peace one develops inner clarity of vision and therefore is not moved solely by fear, emotion, or appearances. Hence, salvation begins with the Son of God who is called "the Prince of Peace" or the principle of peace, if you will. As such, He is also the end of salvation and leads to ultimate peace, so that God even says,

> "They will not hurt or destroy in all My holy mountain,
> For the earth will be full of the knowledge of the LORD
> As the waters cover the sea."
>
> Isa 11:9 NAU

The Master also says, "My peace I give to you..." as the one safeguard against evil and death. A person of peace and true divine peace is truly unmoved by the ebb and flow of things in time. It may seem contradictory to our senses, but the man of peace is moved by the problems of the world to make peace. He is moved by a vision of the inner reality of the being of God and from that vision, he lives out a peace which transmutes the world without agitating the inner tranquility that frames restorative resonance of the divine rest. Those who are overly moved by the imperfections of the world lose peace and hence lose their authentic power for peace. It is ironic that by focusing on that place of peace in the inner being of the Holy One, where it seems they care not for the world in all of its movements, they are able to be peacemakers. A peacemaker, in order to be used, must have peace inwardly to dwell in that realm in which they have overcome the necessity of fate and the compulsions of evil.

It is because they are reborn from the non-agitated realm of God that true peacemakers are called the sons of God. Peace is the true essence of divinity—it is the power to become the sons of God which is spoken of in John 1:12. Indeed, Paul even connects peace with holiness,

> [14] "Pursue peace with all men, and the sanctification without which no one will see the Lord.
>
> [15] See to it that no one comes short of the grace of God; that no root of bitterness springing up causes

trouble, and by it many be defiled;"

Heb 12:14-15 NAU

We see here that peace with all men is the root of sanctification because that peace must be within. When our hearts are at peace, we carry holiness and our eyes can see God. But the lack of peace is the root of bitterness and defilement. Look at the progression: peace lays the groundwork for sanctification and cleanses the soul's eyes. On the negative side, the lack of peace defiles and blinds the soul's eyes from seeing God. It is the spring of trouble. Thus, peace can be used as technology for beholding the face above and the face below and, yes, for deification. In peace, serenity, and harmonic integrality, we become more like God for He creates not out of inner restlessness but from rest.

> peace with all men is the root of sanctification

Rather than look at the essence of God from the perspective of peace, it has been common to look at it from the perspective of power. While power has been so analyzed and pushed as the ultimate mark of divine life and manifestation, the scriptures seldom push the power to make war and dominate as even the power to do miracles and signs is the essence of the inner life of God. This is not to say that God is not powerful, but that our definition of power is not a description of the inner life of God. God demonstrates His power so that humanity, the nations, and Israel may know that Yahweh is God and seek Him and come to Him. However, if warfare and all the acts we call signs and wonders were the definition of the inner being of God, then the Olympian gods would have been more "god" than God and the gods of the nations with all the lying wonders would be God. The center of the being we call our God is peace. The fundamental quest has been to make peace and to give peace. The only reason He became man was to make peace. He came to do this because it is intrinsic to His being, to the divine self-definition. The creation of the world came from that peace. Though shattered by the fall of man, it nonetheless remains the eternal goal of God's heart. His peace can only be restored by sons. Thus, the peacemakers shall be called the sons of God because only sons can restore to humanity the peace that is intrinsic to the Godhead. Simply, they are sons of peace - the result of heavenly harmonization, and they carry God's peacemaking capacity within them.

8TH BEATITUDE

8th Beatitude, Blessed are they which are persecuted for righteousness' sake

Blessed are they which are persecuted for righteousness' sake: for theirs is the Kingdom of Heaven

Matthew 5:10 NAU

Those who are persecuted "for righteousness' sake," if they do so consciously, gain an immediate mystical cognition and are able to unleash timeless instantiations of the creaturely goodness which is veiled within creation.

When one suffers for "righteousness' sake" one may end up activating generational leverage for humanity; we can see this in many who have suffered for righteousness' sake. Such suffering engages and unveils the hidden aspects of the heaven and the confluence and flow of the birth of worlds. It speaks to the very idea of self-sacrifice as the basis of the birth of worlds. The power of suffering for righteousness' sake is that it enormously increases the faculty of compassion and love in the one who allows it to take its course and it also strengthens one's concentrative capacity to transmute the world for which for one suffers.

This "for righteousness' sake" takes more than mere human alignment with suffering. It is not a victimhood, a passive letting oneself suffer. It is a conscious engagement of the whole being to serve as the channel for the flow of the life of God into the world in spite of the disdain of the very world for which one suffers.

This capacity to bear the pain for suffering that results from one's good or righteous acts or for being righteous is much more painful, yet it expresses the Sacramentality of the life connected to the heart of God. This suffering to bring forth righteousness in humanity is counter-intuitive to how we seem to be wired. Questions concerning why the righteous suffer, why the good are often persecuted, why there is evil in the world, and why a good God allows evil, are almost irrelevant here, if I may be so sacrilegious. It begs the real question: "How should we suffer as men and women created by freedom for freedom?" This question is at the heart of human desire to escape suffering and herein lies the weakness of man—why he fails to engage the suffering of another, and why so many do not see the alchemical power in their suffering and live in the bane of constant complaint and external focus. Here we see that Jesus is not Job. He is not bemoaning the reality of suffering by raising a tirade against his friend and shaking his fist at a supposedly unjust God. That would be the denial of the Divine in human suffering. To suffer as gods and change the human condition as God's offspring is

> conscious engagement of the whole being

the intrinsic power of the intentional suffering focused on birthing righteousness into the world.

So the question, as I have said, is "How shall we suffer?" The ancillary question is "For what do we suffer?" I think that when the question is asked thus, it raises for us the issue of suffering consciously and our capacity to use suffering as an instrument of ecstatic technology for world transformation. As such, this "for righteousness' sake" is a tool for transmuting the various forces within human beings that pulls us toward perpetual destruction. Within the one who suffers for righteousness' sake is the singular creative burst of energy that charges toward the redemption of someone within the vicinity of suffering for righteousness' sake . As Stephen's suffering penetrates the hardened heart of a Saul or the suffering of Jesus tears through the hardened crust of the warrior criminal's heart and leads him to cry out, "Truly this was the Son of God!" Suffering for righteousness' sake activates and absorbs spiritual "at-one-ment" and distributes it from the soul of the sufferer into the sphere of human consciousness. It comes from an altered state of consciousness whereby the sufferer has immediate access to the hidden scrolls of God codes within creation. Their suffering is able to create new realities, make it available in the context of their suffering and echo its possibility long after they are gone. In such people is the awareness of living which can be harnessed to recalibrate any space, place, or time. Their suffering unleashes the yet uncreated idea of human potential and transformation, and it engages the edge of the Divine mind, forcing open the eyes of the heart of those who would rather gaze with the eyes of flesh at those who suffer for righteousness' sake.

For righteousness' sake is not merely suffering for being different or acting differently or even acting in righteousness and receiving typical human disdain, but rather, it is a righteous embrace of suffering based on reflective consciousness. It flows from the meditative penetration of the heart into the experience of suffering with an end to transformation of the perpetrators and the environment in which the desire to cause another to suffer grows. For righteousness' sake implies that, contemplatively, the sufferer clearly understands the reason for suffering and yet is still led to choose it rationally, knowing fully well the personal cost. The teleology (explanation of something in terms of the purpose it serves rather than its cause) of suffering is thought to be worth the present pain and cost. It is in contemplating the cost and yet choosing suffering in spite of it that the blessedness of which the Master speaks dwells. Only such people are blessed. That He was led as a lamb to the slaughter, and He opened not his mouth does not mean that his suffering was not chosen and contemplated with the aim of human transformation in mind.

The suffering of anyone for righteousness' sake is a deeper language of the cosmos and creation, in which all its signs, metaphors, symbols, and occlusion communicate that singular divine intent pointing at the transformation and transmutation of the human being. This transformative suffering and self-giving enhancement which often enters into human experience is represented in images, metaphors, and symbols of sacrificial process and divine beings, even in the relationship between parents and children. So suffering for righteousness' sake is intrinsic in the way the worlds are sustained and kept in their ever-moving cycles. Here, in the choice to suffer for righteousness' sake, an efficacy is activated for one in their usefulness for the transmutation of the world, thus presenting one's life as a sacramental object by virtue of it having being identified with the sacramental life of Jesus Christ. The need to suffer not as a slave but as a son is the distinction between transformative suffering and the profanity of irreformable suffering, like suicide. Suffering for righteousness can be said to be sacramental in that it is capable of mediating the original intention of the Divine to bring the world to completion.

The capacity to bear the pain of suffering that results from good shows that it is never the persecutor who determines what righteousness is. The divine relevance of one's suffering is not determined by his/her detractors; rather, it is determined from within based on why and how one chooses to go through suffering. This means in one way that the blessedness draws from something beyond the present suffering. It's not just that present suffering is the measure of future blessedness. The truth is that suffering for righteousness' sake always draws from an unlimited future. The distinction implicit in the Lord's statement for "righteousness sake" is meant to make it clear that He is not talking of those who get caught in their web of wickedness of being coldhearted and murderous or those who interpret righteousness as an affront to their sense of decency and decorum. We have seen this enough in history when those have subjected others to oppression and death are so quick to cry foul when they get what they deserve. How quickly humans forget their own wickedness when the table is turned!

This righteousness must be in the direction of pouring divinity back into creation and not just in terms of securing one's own fate by suffering for one's goodness, whatever that may be. It is not the claim of innocence or presumed righteousness which the sufferer shall manifest that makes the person blessed. For long after they are gone, men, women and children will reach up to harvest from the tree of their life and be blessed. It can also be said that often it is not the rightness or the wrongness of the matter that elicits suffering, but more often than not, it is its affront to culturally-accepted norms or the desire to abrogate what is right that men may discard boundaries and misdirect humanity.

In the present day, it is not the necessarily an affront to cultural mores that is really the issue, but the desire of men to turn secret evil into a public norm, flip humanity on its head, and discard its nature for that which works towards its extinction. It is typically laced with divine standards which society deems impossible to keep or, if anyone does adhere to them, they believe affronts god by presumed perfection. Righteousness' sake does not necessarily equate universal judgment but exists in the context of an assumed more that the persecuted seem to have broken or breached. In my experience of persecution in this context, those who do the persecuting give metaphorical linguistic definition to the victim of their persecution. Such definitions are often infected by falsehood about the nature of righteousness. However, those who suffer have an intuitive grasp of the power of suffering and its power to shape the future of human thought. Righteousness' sake reflects an apparent, intrinsic, or inherent mode of being which is not accidental or coincidental, but rather consists in a willed mode of being. It is a response to real life in the context of one's conviction, inconveniencing the pretended hypocritical neatness of culturally bound assumption, whatever that may be. It may even take the form of revolutionary rewriting of society's psychic engagement with the Divine nature with a view to how that life is to be manifested in human communion with one another.

Those who suffer for righteousness' sake reflect the union of the name YHVH-Elohim—the union of the sun and the moon. In fact, it is said by some of the ancients that the moon subjected itself to the light of the sun by virtue of the work that must be done by Adam to bring together the grades of life. "He that suffers for righteousness' sake" thus brings the HEH and righteousness together. Suffering with divine intention is ultimately a tool for union, helping us transcend our present circumstances, transmute our current mode of existence, and translate its inadequacies by divine synthesis into something far greater than the immediate suffering. Thus Paul says,

> [18] For I consider that the sufferings of this present time are not worthy to be compared with the glory that is to be revealed to us.
>
> [19] For the anxious longing of the creation waits eagerly for the revealing of the sons of God.
>
> [20] For the creation was subjected to futility, not of its own will, but because of Him who subjected it, in hope
>
> [21] that the creation itself also will be set free from its slavery to corruption into the freedom of the glory of the children of God.

²² For we know that the whole creation groans and suffers the pains of childbirth together until now.

²³ And not only this, but also we ourselves, having the first fruits of the Spirit, even we ourselves groan within ourselves, waiting eagerly for our adoption as sons, the redemption of our body.

Rom 8:18-23 NAS

For righteousness' sake speaks to the intention of the sufferer or persecuted both in terms of the original intent of their life actions, which determines their behavior, and the teleology of their mode being which brings about the suffering (i.e., what the act intends that leads to persecution or suffering). What was the act meant to produce in the first place? Suffering for righteousness' sake is the binding of the Bohu/tohu to create life-sustaining worlds. It is the binding of chaos and formlessness by the blood and tears of the sufferer whose composition engenders a creative, pioneering process — such cannot be done without sacrifice.

There is a right way to engage suffering. Suffering the right way creates the codes for life in this world and the world to come. Underlying the very existence of the world is the divine embrace of joyful suffering. One who embraces no manner of suffering cannot act in a way that life emerges from his or her life. In fact, it is not possible to cause life to emerge from the primordial matter of the universe without sacrifice, so the ancients have tried to tell us. Suffering for righteousness' sake can cause the soul to cleave to the source of creation and to align it with the original divine intent.

> YHVH

Suffering for righteousness' sake must also include the sacrifice and giving of the self as one studies the word of God. Very few mysteries are hidden from the one who suffers for righteousness' sake. When one suffers for righteousness' sake, their whole being is opened to the wondrous light of creation and the Creator.

When suffering comes, we judge it, we judge the sufferer, we compare ourselves with others, and we try to dissect the reason for suffering. Others around who see us suffer quite often than not want to ask, "What heinous sin have you committed that makes you a candidate of such suffering?" Nonetheless, it is not why we suffer, for suffer we must, that is our greatest question to be answered, but rather how we shall we suffer. Our posture toward the intent and purpose of our suffering either allows righteousness to show up or can birth bitterness which reaps mayhem for us and those around us.

Recall that righteousness is demonstrating those things that enhance human life by causing the divine life and purpose for humanity to manifest through the instrumentation of our suffering and how we experience it in our inward nature. To what end do we suffer? The end we have in mind as we go through suffering can open up the Kingdom of Heaven to us and to those around us who participate vicariously in our suffering. Indeed, it might even open up the Kingdom of Heaven for those who mete out that suffering upon us, wittingly or unwittingly. Suffering for righteousness' sake may cause us to experience things beyond our conscripted and structured reality, allowing us to observe reality from a different vantage point. In suffering for righteousness' sake, one may gain a fresh perspective of observation: observing oneself, themselves, and perhaps even observing others observe opaque reality who are unable to pierce the veil of illusionary "reality," spiritually speaking.

Suffering for righteousness' sake is one way to recalibrate and rectify creation. Whenever one undertakes suffering for righteousness' sake, one exhibits a mirror image of the divine life because it gives clues to the divine suffering which sustains worlds both in the direction of the "Il tempore" as well as in the direction of the redemptive movement towards the future. Suffering in this case works rectification backward and forward. Any suffering when observed from the perspective of righteousness, whether it is the righteousness' that is the result of suffering or the righteousness that gives rise to the suffering, shows what the soul is made of. When we suffer with the intent of releasing righteousness, it reveals more than philosophical contemplation about the soul - it shows the level of the growth of God within that soul. We may live a life focused on the extrinsic as long as occasions do not arise that may cause us to suffer for righteousness sake. Suffering may also lead us to an extrinsic focus, blaming others, circumstances and God. However, it is hard to focus externally while suffering for righteousness' sake, since this particular kind of suffering calls for interiority and inner reflection (with all due respect to George Gurdjieff), a type of personal identification with divine suffering especially as revealed in the incarnation of God in Jesus Christ. The mystery of this statement from the Lord Jesus Christ is the revelation of precreation sacrifice based on the will of substantiated divinity when the upper body of the Most High establishes the lower world by sacrifice and creation as an altar from whence wisdom, understanding, knowledge and love flow. From that original example of the Holy One in which He gave himself for righteousness' sake so that he might bring forth the righteous who form the foundation of the worlds, the Master draws and says, "Blessed are those who suffer for righteousness' sake." For righteousness' sake, God suffered Himself to withdraw and suffer hiddenness so that the righteous might appear. It was for righteousness' sake that He created the worlds. The righteous are the foundation of worlds.

How many of you have ever suffered? The scripture says that God, in order to perfect or to bring us to salvation, made the champion, allowed the champion of our faith to suffer. The word suffering is a terrible word. We actually use it to attack God. We ask, "If God is good, why is there so much suffering in the world?" I have my biblical reasons for arguing that all the sufferings in the world were not created by God. Some of it was created by us. God didn't create suffering. Human activities create suffering. Let's just deal with this. "The champion of our faith was perfected through suffering." (Hebrews 2:10) It goes on to say that God did not come into the world to help angels, but to help people with flesh and blood. In other words, God's main purpose in coming as a human being is to participate in our suffering. If God wanted not to suffer, He would have become an angel. There's no reason for angels to suffer. So the intrinsic principle is for God to become a human being to participate in human suffering, to participate in the world.

Now I want to make a distinction between suffering caused by people and suffering that just happens in the world, what I call intentional suffering for the purpose of transformation and transmutation. You cannot often choose which suffering comes to you, but you can choose how you suffer.

The way the world is, things just happen, right? That's the way the world is. But you can choose how you suffer. For it was fitting for Him, for whom are all things, and through whom are all things, in bringing many sons to glory, to perfect the author of their salvation through sufferings. (Hebrews 2:10)

For most people, suffering is almost like a four-letter word. It's almost like a curse word. People don't want to talk about it. If you see somebody suffering you ask, "God why are they suffering?" Your whole issue is that suffering is fundamentally bad. I have a lot to say about that.

In Hebrews 2:11, the scripture says, "For both He who sanctifies and those who are sanctified are all from one Father." That translation is wrong. The original language says "He that sanctifies and the ones that are sanctified are one." In other words, when you suffer, God suffers! If the One who sanctifies and the one that is sanctified are one, it means when the sanctified is suffering, the Sanctifier also suffers. So you never suffer alone. I know there are different kinds of suffering, but let's focus on what Jesus meant when He said, "Blessed are those who suffer for righteousness' sake..."

> People do not like suffering

Any suffering that comes your way can become a suffering for righteousness' sake. Remember, it's not the fact that you suffer, it's how you suffer. It's how you receive the suffering and how you engage the suffering. So Jesus

Christ came into the world, knowing clearly and explicitly that it was going to cost Him suffering.

What does it mean to suffer for righteousness' sake? It means to engage suffering in such a way that it transmutes humanity from its current position to a new position. Any pain and suffering that you engage intentionally, you need to look at it from a cosmic perspective, not mainly from a personal perspective. You must look at it from the perspective of humanity as a whole. Anything you go through that you engage that way becomes suffering for righteousness' sake. How? Because when you suffer rightly, you also help transmute humanity. You help other human beings get to their own position of freedom. Your suffering is never in vain!

You know when you're going through it you think this is all about you. "Why me? Poor me! Why me?" However, maybe how you go through suffering would be different if you looked at your situation and said, "I'm embracing this intentionally because in my going through this, the world is rectified. Humanity is raised up a little bit higher because I'm going through this." It's a hard thing to tell people because no one likes to suffer. That's how we are. People do not like suffering which is why engaging suffering intentionally with a clear-mindedness is the greatest way of expressing your freedom from slavery to your human nature. How you suffer is a revelation of how free you are!

You don't want to suffer as a slave. You want to suffer as a free person. And the ultimate example of what it means to engage suffering from the position of freedom is the person of Jesus. His suffering and ultimate death on the cross didn't just "happen" to Him. But even if it had just "happened" to Him, how He experienced it helped to transform who you are. How He engaged it is the reason you are here today, right? Some of you reading this today have been through so many things, but you have no idea that having intentionally engaged with your suffering, somebody else has been healed. How we engage our suffering determines whether our neighbor is free.

Jesus said you have to suffer for righteousness' sake. What is righteousness? Is righteousness merely a moral stance? Is it merely an ethical position where you make rules and regulations? The Bible says something very powerful that actually removes all of that religious jargon—not that morality or ethics are not important. Ultimately, the scripture says we are the righteousness of God through Christ. (2 Corinthians 5:21)

In the final analysis, righteousness is about people. It is humanity who benefits from suffering for righteousness' sake. If you suffer merely for morality and it doesn't transform humanity, your suffering is wasted. If you're truly moral, truly ethical, and truly "spiritual," then your suffering is always directed to lifting up other human beings. Why do you do the things you do for your children? Why do you go through what you go through in spite of all the pain they cause you? If it was about morality, you would have abandoned them a long time ago. If it was only about the perfection of your children, you would have walked away a long time ago. It's about the person. And the person is the righteousness of God. So for righteousness' sake means for humanity's sake. Therefore, if you can suffer intentionally for humanity's sake per the Christian scripture, you will now be raising people who are righteous. And if the Bible is true and the righteous are the foundation of the world, then by your suffering you will be rectifying the foundation of creation. Again, your suffering is not in vain! It's only in vain if you suffer as a slave.

Let's think about this in terms of sacrificial systems. The high priest or the priest of every religion makes a sacrifice. They sacrifice an animal, but the animal is a representation of the priest. For those of you who are into the Jewish religion, how do Jews sacrifice? The priest puts his hands on the animal, thereby transferring the totality of his being into the animal. Instead of him dying on the altar, he puts his essence on the animal so the animal dies. So every true priest must learn how to suffer intentionally. When I was in school it was a big deal when we talked about redemptive suffering. People got all upset. They didn't want to talk about redemptive offering—they say it's a way people oppress other people. But I'm not talking about oppression. I'm talking about a willing and intentional engagement of personal suffering. If you don't engage suffering, it's not going to go away just because you don't like it. The stuff you're going through now is not going to go away just because you close your eyes like an ostrich and put your head in the ground. When you put your head back up, it's still going to be there. So what you do is learn how to engage it intentionally so that your suffering becomes transmutative. It becomes a power that repairs not just your world, but the world of the people around you.

When Jesus says for righteousness' sake, it's more than just you aligning yourself with suicidal, sadomasochistic processes. Nobody's asking you to be a sadist. That's not what this is about. It's not you just deciding you're going to go hurt yourself. That's why suicide is not suffering. I understand there are chemical reasons for why people do it, but 90% of the people who kill themselves do it out of cowardice because they don't want to engage suffering. I understand the psychological stuff. That's part of my degree. I understand what that is. However, the reason we complain about many of the things going on in our lives is because we don't want to engage the reality of our situation. And I can push that even further. Why do people do drugs? To escape. All the great gurus and all the great religious leaders will tell you that creating an intentional engagement of life is actually much more powerful than escaping through drugs. It has its own capacity to help you handle reality.

There is nothing in this world that God made in this world that is as powerful as your will and your intention. Just you engaging something out sheer will and intention can turn things around. The will to live is greater than the will to die. Haven't you heard of people where the doctor has said they are going to die, but their response is, "No, I'm not dying." Slowly, slowly the person is restored to health. The will to die is a secondary, not a primary principle. A conscious engagement of the whole being to serve as the channel of the flow of the life of God is what you do when you deliberately choose to engage somebody else's suffering and make it your personal suffering. When you do that, you become a conscious channel by which God flows into the humanity. Any Christian who doesn't like that has to remove Jesus Christ from their faith because the foundation of your faith is that someone chose to suffer on your behalf—not just to suffer personally, but to engage in your suffering as a way of allowing the flow of divinity into your being.

I know you're probably thinking, "I'm suffering too much." True. I can never in my life tell you suffering is not painful. That would be false and really terrible thing to say. Your suffering is real. It's not an illusion. The pain is real. However, the moment you make up your mind that you're engaging this for not just the transformation of your life, but of other people's lives, for the transformation of the world, for the transformation of the future, it changes the way you experience it. Try it and see.

What happens if you're trying to do something nice and people turn on you? There's not a person here that's not been there. People turn on you. It's painful, right? But the result depends on how you embrace the principle. If you start going through the process of self-pity, nobody has a remedy for you. Not even God has the remedy for you. How many times has He answered you when you say why me? Does He come down to you and say, "I want to explain to you why it is you"? God is always silent when you do that. Your answer is in a deliberate intentional willful engagement for the purpose of allowing your life to become sacramental so that by engaging the suffering you repeat what God Himself does when He comes into the world. Through this type of engagement, you actually become God in the flesh.

So then, God created the world according to Christianity by giving God's life. Jesus Christ is the lamb of God that was slain before the foundation of the world. Therefore, this world is the result of the giving of the divine life. Redemption is the giving of divine life. I want to challenge you when I say that even the suffering and death of God is incomplete without your own suffering. The only way it will be complete without you is if you were never created. But you're here. How do we deal with this reality of suffering? Think about Joseph, Mary's husband. Wouldn't you call what Joseph was going through suffering? He was present when Jesus Christ is born into the world. Then somebody wants to kill the baby. The baby doesn't know what's happening, but the father and the mother have to make a decision to uproot themselves to go to another country and be among foreign people. If they did not embrace that intentionally, we would have a problem with the person of Jesus. It wasn't just the fact that Jesus was born into the world to suffer. It's the fact that the people He came through had to go through suffering in order to make His sacrifice a possibility. Without Joseph and Mary, without the people who helped Him along the way, who suffered for Him, His suffering would have not been real. The Magis decided to take a longer way home. Joseph decided to remove himself from his job and his family and go to Egypt. Mary, shortly after giving birth, climbed on top of a donkey and traveled all the way from Jerusalem to upper Egypt close to Ethiopia where there were a lot of Jews. The woman Mary and the man Joseph suffered to make manifest the reality of the messiah's appearance. Somebody suffered to make the future possibility of the suffering of Jesus a reality, which then resulted in your redemption.

It's not the fact that you suffer that is your problem. It's how you suffer and how you perceive what you're going through. You can't read that story and just talk about the suffering of Jesus. In the person of Christ, is the culmination of the suffering of all humanity. His death on the cross dealt with something about you, but it didn't finish everything. We quote His last words all the time: "It is finished." Yes, it is finished, that is, the payment for the sin. Yet your own suffering and your own sacrifice must then activate the possibility for the people around you to receive what Christ has done. Without your suffering, it's incomplete. I'm sorry to put it that way but guess what? If God wants to save your children, He sends you and they will attack you and say all kinds of stuff against you. Your suffering must complete the process whereby they accept the redemptive principle of Christ. If God wants to heal somebody on the street, He sends you.

> Never discount your own suffering

That person you're trying to heal might be the one that slaps you all over the place and curses you, but that's your suffering for completing the process so that person can participate in the redemptive process.

Never discount your own suffering as if it means nothing. And don't make yourself a victim because every champion must be perfected by suffering. This is so powerful! Sometimes you and I forget that the things that happen to us is actually God calling us to participate in His life. Is God saying to us, "I don't want to do this alone"? Is God saying to you, "I know it's painful, but how are you and I going to be in union with each other if I don't allow you to go through the same thing I go through every day?" Take heart! God is not unfair and will not forget all your sufferings. He is in that suffering with you. He's in that struggle with you. Suffering for righteousness' sake is a tool for the transmuting of the various forces of nature within human beings. It's a way by which we are pulled perpetually away from destruction. When we suffer, we think that is the end of the world. But really, if we tune our perspective so that the suffering is seen as a technology for transformation, we pull the world away from destruction. Let me give you a biblical example. Remember when Stephen was getting stoned? Do you realize that even while he was being killed, his perspective and what he saw at the moment of his suffering is what transformed and transmuted the lives of the people who were actually hurting him. He saw heaven open. And the young man that was there a few days later had a vision of heaven because the sufferer saw heaven and transmuted in his suffering. Who knows how many people who were around Stephen were transformed by God because his perspective of his suffering was different. We can talk about Jesus all day long, but there are human beings that have done the same thing. By the way, you do the same thing with your children, with your friends, with your wife, with your husband. And you do it until there's a transformation and sometimes you don't even realize it's your suffering. Open your eyes and you see how much your struggle has transformed the people around you. But God is such a God that He hides everything.

Jesus tears through the crust of the hardened warrior criminal's heart and leads him to cry out, "Truly this is the Son of God!" How did He do it? The way He suffered. The guy didn't cry because Jesus was cursing everybody from the cross. He watched how Jesus suffered and it resulted in his shouting, "This is the Son of God!" Suffering for righteousness' sake activates and absorbs and distributes spiritual essences even to those who disdain the sufferer. When you suffer rightly, you even open up your whole being to the possibility of altered states of consciousness. Your suffering can transmute and transform the way you look at the world and allow you to look deeper. Some sufferings are shocks, right? If you allow the shock to register, your consciousness gets transmuted and altered. It's a tool. If you see your discomfort and the things that happen in your life as a tool for self-transformation or self-alteration, it expands the things you can do in life. People may accost you every month, every week, or even every day. How you handle what they say determines whether you get stuck where you are or you create new realities. You can make available to the people around you the essence of God by the way you handle how people treat you and the deck the world deals you. Every time you go through difficulties, see it as you repeating what God did to create the world in your own personal life. Understand that there are some things that God is trying to birth in you. Maybe there's things inside of you that God's trying to manifest. Most people won't even pray unless they're suffering. It's important to understand how your pain is a tool for not just transforming your world, but for opening up and securing the future. The greatest example of this is women. A woman goes through a lot of suffering to have a child. For what? To secure the future. Not just her future, but the future of humanity. Because we see them everywhere, we think it's common, but it's not common. God embedded those things in the simple processes of life so we would understand that our struggles are not in vain.

The scripture says,

> ...and when you suffer, rejoice and be exceedingly glad. (Matthew 5:12)

I was wondering why Psalms is included in the passage. I realized that the people who picked the text were including the Psalms of praise to let you know the eight processes or the eight dimensions of praise above, the seven dimensions of praise in the atmosphere, and the eight dimensions of praise among men that allows for the transformation of human experience which leads to the transformation of the world. The way people handle suffering has to do with the level of intrinsic praise and joy that is embedded in their being. What did Jesus say? You are blessed if you suffer. And if people persecute you, rejoice and be exceedingly glad because the antidote is in carrying joy, and the only way you can carry joy and that sort of power is if you understand that your experience is birthing an alternate future. Once you get clear what your life can give birth to, your mode of experiencing changes. Your suffering will bring forth fruit beyond what you think. Praise the Lord.

The Beatific Life

9TH BEATITUDE

9th Beatitude, Identified with the crucified: Blessed are ye when men shall revile

"Blessed are ye when men shall revile you and persecute you, and shall say all manner of evil against you falsely, for my sake"

We move from "righteousness' sake" to "for my sake" which also equals "for my name's sake." One could argue that for righteousness' sake is the same as for my sake and " for my name's sake."

However, the phrase "for my name's sake" is specifically about the person and being of God. In the idea of facing mans revile, persecution, evil speech, and false testimony, my name's sake is embedded with this secret that the one who goes through these trials "for my name's sake" brings the transcendent God into immanency.

The idea of "for my name's sake" throws insight into how a person can ground the esoteric knowledge or abstract Knowledge of God in the human context. The impact of manifesting the Name or *shemot* (שֵׁמוֹת) is twofold. First, the one experiencing revile and persecution for my name's sake becomes the embodiment of the name. Second, knowing the name in this way confers on this person the true image of the complex movement of divinity upon the creation. In other words, they become the tower, the temple, and the altar of the presence of the Holy One in every undertaking of their ordinary daily life. The one who suffers for His name's sake embodies the name of YHVH in all its permutations: YHVH, EHYH, AHVH, AHAVAH. In this way, they form the root of the tree of life that diffuses light, empowers creation and enlivens it. The four roots with the outgrowth reach downward into the one who suffers for His Name's sake (Israel and all the righteous who fear and love the Holy one), connecting them to the Holy One and drawing from His depth (Blessed be). This depth that they access is not a casting down, but a lifting up to the supernal life of the Holy One. All these are caught up into the names of Salvation Yod Heh Shin Vav Heh (יהשוה) summarized in the appellative symbolic expression עִמָּנוּאֵל read as Imma-Nu-El (Mother is in EL=mother re-enters the father and Humanity shall be one). The root names YHVH, EHYH, AHVH ELHM result in the flow of salvation in creation from which spread the strength of the Holy One to the nations from Israel. This strength has always entered through the root names. The nations can enter only when the name of names enters which is the name of the messiah. When that name and its true meaning is revealed and accepted by Israel, then shall the throne of the Holy One descend and Zion

> only the truth about God will keep us from rebelling

shall shine by the glory of the throne and the whole world shall come to it. Then Zion shall replicate itself in all worlds and rectify myriads of worlds. Those who suffer for the name's sake become the fulcrum for this replication. It is why Israel has always suffered from the hands of Gentiles for the "His Name's sake." Today, the righteous suffer for that name's sake.

Of course, each name of God contains a deep secret which creates openings of interconnectivity between worlds. As the whole structure of the Torah in its written form and its oral practice embodies the breath of the Holy One, each true name of God in all languages grows out these roots and carries with it the outflow of the essence of the Holy One. In Israel, the roots give forth thirteen outflows which move from their rung into myriads of worlds until all are filled with the glory of the Holy One as the waters covers the sea.

So when one undertakes to revile, persecute, speak evil and falsify against another, "for my name's sake" has put an axe to the four roots of the names in the life of the righteous. Because these four names sustain the righteous in this world and the world to come, whoever attacks the righteous in the four ways enumerated by the Master, attacks the world to come and hinders its manifestation in this world. Not only does it mean that they hinder the world to come, but there is an underlying attack on the name and person of God. Such attacks are for God's sake or the sake of the Messiah because both the YHVH and His Messiah are truth. As is said, "O YHVH God of truth" (Psalm 31:5). אמת , the Hebrew word for truth, combines the first letter of the otiyot (א), the middle letter of the glyph (מ), and the final letter of the glyph (ת). Thus an attack on a righteous person through lies is an attack on the Aleph the instruction of the Holy One, an attempt to undo the foundation of creation for Aleph is the hidden source of Creation. Furthermore, the Holy One Himself is called the "beginning" which is Aleph. The very makeup of the first letter has the same numeric value as the name of the Holy One (Yod VAV Yod). Therefore, anyone who speaks falsely of the righteous attacks the truth and, in so doing, attacks the name and person of Yahweh. It is as though that one has cast a veil upon the manifestation of the messiah and kept him from coming into the present world.

The Messiah is the full manifestation of the Holy One in creation. Since the righteous are the foundation of the worlds, a falsehood against a righteous person is the undoing of the foundation of creation. The Mem (מ) in the middle of the word truth in the Hebrew glyph represents the womb and sustaining fluid of creation or the waters of life that flow from the belly of the righteous which sustains humanity and creation as whole. Falsifying the testimony of the righteous is an attack on YHVH, representing the fours rivers flowing from Eden which sustain the life of the world to come. The truth of the righteous serves as a conduit in this present world. It is by the embodied stream of the life of the righteous that the Holy One causes Olam HaBa (עוֹלָם הַבָּא) (the world to come) to become Olam HaZeh (עוֹלָם הַבָּא), the world that is. The complaints of the wicked or the people against the Holy One or against His righteous ones such as Moses is what embitters the waters of creation and causes sickness and death.

The Mem represents in the word truth or "emeth" (אמת) the waters or mayim (מַיִם) of Massah and Meribah where the of the sons of Israel quarrel with Moses and the Lord. It is said that "because they tested the LORD, saying, 'Is the LORD among us, or not?'", it can also be said that the Lord tested the hearts of the leaders and the people (Exodus 17:7). The next verse of the chapter says, "Those were the waters of Meribah, because the sons of Israel contended with the LORD, and He proved Himself holy among them." For this reason it seems that the truth of their hearts was revealed as to what it would be like with them occupying the land of God's contentment and liberty. When we are raised by grace to become like God, will it go to our head, and we rebel? We do not find any serious rebellion against the Father in Numbers 24. What we see is the hidden truth of the heart which has not yet come to fruition but will once the journey is over, and they are established in their Divine position. In fact, according to Numbers 20:24, God insisted that "Aaron shall be gathered to his people; for he shall not enter the land which I have given to the sons of

Israel, because you rebelled against My command at the waters of Meribah."

During strife, only the truth we have imbibed about God will keep us from rebelling against God's command to treat Him as holy before the eyes of the world." At the water, the place of trouble or of supply are in the waters of Meribah of Kadesh in the wilderness of Zin. God's Thummim and Urim that belongs to the godly man is the truth of God that sits as the light upon the seats of the heart and head. His Thummim and Urim prove him when things are not going well at the waters of their trouble, whether it comes from supply or lack, from good times, or even from the complacence of satisfaction after a hard-earned victory. Everyone has that place of Massah and Meribah where God will contend with them. Do you believe that no matter how rough the waters, YHVH is the one who says, "You called in trouble, and I rescued you; I answered you in the hiding place of thunder; I proved you at the waters of Meribah. Selah" (Psalm 81:7). Blessed is the one who does not harden his heart in that day but endures for His sake who does "not harden *their* hearts, as at Meribah, As in the day of Massah in the wilderness" (Psalm 95:8), but for YHVH's sake, stays the course. Because the Mem is both a birthing channel or a river flowing from its source and also a closed lake or spring, it represents the heart and its outflowing content. Massah and Meribah may be looked at as the two extremities.

The final letter of emth (אמת)is Tav which serves as a gateway leading from death to life. In a sense, it is the ending that does not end because it is a walking door, so to speak. It is the end that leads to the beginning-less beginning. It the place back to before the foundation of the world which allows those who pass through it to be able to recalibrate creation. As such the high priest passed through the ת to cause Israel to return to the beginning-less beginning where Israel can, by her prayers and her sacrifices before the arrival of the messiah, cause the world to begin again. Truth is the instrument by which the world is recreated. The righteous as the embodiment of truth are the carriers of terrestrial and celestial renewability and repair. Truth is the technology for

Tikun Olam. This passage draws the esoteric hiddenness of what is being said when people revile and persecute whose who follow the LORD. First of all, they suffer for goodness counted by the persecutor as evil. Secondly, they suffer for beauty counted as ugliness. Thirdly, they suffer for glory counted as shame. Fourthly, they may be put to death which is an attack on the immortality of God - ultimately, human death means the removal of God from the presence of the wicked.

When one suffers for something that bears the name of God or the Messiah of righteousness, one strengthens the name of the LORD and causes creation to draw from the root causing hope to grow whereby the faces of suffering humanity look upward and the face of the Holy One gazes downward and inwardly through the tree of life shaking its leaves of abundance to bring healing into the world. The face of the persecuted, reviled, vilified, and falsely accused, illuminates the line of glory, beauty, and mercy. The name for which they suffer is the Name that blesses, the Name that keeps, the Name of the countenance that lifts Israel and all the righteous up. That name shines in order to radiate and cause the face of the holy ones to shine. It is the name that pours out grace upon Israel and the fearer of YHVH. It is the Name of the face of peace. The one who does the four things that Master Jesus spoke of against the righteous or anyone who falls into what the Master lists above attacks the garment of God's holy name because, since He made man in His image and likeness, the Holy One uses the righteous to cover and reveal His name in creation.

The concept of "for my name's sake" is drawn from the idea that the Messiah is the image of the Holy One, for it is said that in Him, the fullness of the Godhead dwells (Colossians 2:9). He is also the expressed image of the Godhead. The idea is that if one is connected and entangled with the Holy One, an attack on them is an indirect attack on the God whom they worship and to whom they are so connected.

10TH BEATITUDE

10th Beatitude, You are in Good Company: for so persecuted they the prophets

Rejoice and be exceedingly glad:
for great is your reward in Heaven:
for so persecuted they the prophets
which were before you.

The blessedness of being persecuted is not what God will do in the future as a result of being reviled and persecuted "for my sake." Rather this blessedness is immediate and makes accessible the company that one will keep both in this world and the world to come. True, one will spend eternity with and have access to the Divine. The twist here is to be in the Good Company of those who have suffered similar ignominy. So rather than cry over such persecution, they are admonished to develop an inner landscape of rejoicing and exceeding gladness: "for great is your reward in heaven; for so persecuted they the prophets which were before you."

> great *is* your reward in heaven

It is worth noting that it does not say, "great *shall be* your reward in heaven" but "great *is* your reward in heaven." This allows those who have gone through the same suffering to access heaven in the immediate and in the future. It is simply an admonishment to eschew bitterness and to develop the technology of uncommon gladness and joy. This allows the persecuted to engage in the immediacy of the joy and gladness of the community of saints. By so doing, they live this life as those who have access now to their reward in heaven.

There is another world which impinges on this world where our reward is present. By the way we respond to this life through all of its difficulties, we have immediate and present access to that reward which *is* there. We don't have to wait to die to access it and those who have are at this moment participating in it. In moments of our suffering and tears, in moments of joy and gladness, in moments of silence and speech, in moments of various engagements with the consciousness of God, we can access that reward. But it is more than a reward - it is an imbuing of the life of heaven in the movement of life here on this plane. It opens up the spirit of just men and women made perfect whose names are written in the Book of Life.

ABOUT THE AUTHOR

Adonijah Okechukwu Ogbonnaya (BA, MATS, MA, Ph.D) is the founder of AACTEV8 International, an Apostolic and Kingdom Ministry which works with the Body of Christ across the globe for Soul Winning, Discipleship, Training, and Equipping the saints in Kingdom mysteries and Kingdom living. Located in Venice, California, Dr. Ogbonnaya (also known as A. Okechukwu or "Dr. O") began preaching the Word of God in the 1970s in his teenage years. He has served as a missionary, church planter, pastor, and professor. Dr. Ogbonnaya has traveled and ministered in over 25 nations in Asia, Africa, Europe, and North and South America with the message of the Gospel of Jesus Christ. He has seen God perform various signs and wonders as He promised in Mark 16:1–17 — the blind receive sight, the deaf hear, the lame walk, the dead are raised, the barren receive the fruit of the womb, lives are transformed and minds renewed. He has focused on helping believers engage the spiritual realities which have been opened up for them in the person of the Lord Jesus Christ. He is a Hebrew-born native of Nigeria, West Africa. He earned his Ph.D and Master's degree in theology and personality and his Master's in religion from Claremont School of Theology. He completed his M.A. in theological studies at Western Evangelical Seminary and his B.A. in religion at Hillcrest Christian College in Canada. He also holds a Ph.D in business publishing.

He is also the presenter of numerous teachings found at: www.aactev8.com.

Dr. Ogbonnaya is married to Pastor Benedicta and is blessed with four wonderful children and grandchildren.

Seraph Creative is a collective of artists, writers, theologians & illustrators who desire to see the body of Christ grow into full maturity, walking in their inheritance as Sons Of God on the Earth.

Sign up to our newsletter to know about the release of the next book in the series, as well as other exciting releases.

Visit our website :
www.seraphcreative.org

www.ingramcontent.com/pod-product-compliance
Lightning Source LLC
Chambersburg PA
CBHW071621080526
44588CB00010B/1211